THE WAR OF CONQUEST

The University of Utah Press
Salt Lake City

THE WAR OF CONQUEST

How It Was Waged Here in Mexico

The Aztecs' Own Story
As Given to Fr. Bernardino de Sahagún,
Rendered into Modern English by

ARTHUR J. O. ANDERSON
and
CHARLES E. DIBBLE

ABOUT THE TRANSLATORS: Charles E. Dibble and Arthur J. O. Anderson are two of the world's leading scholars of the Aztec language and culture. They are co-translators of Fray Bernardino de Sahagún's *General History of the Things of New Spain*, published in thirteen parts by the School of American Research and the University of Utah, available from the University of Utah Press.

ABOUT THE ILLUSTRATIONS: The illustrations and the selected paragraphs in Nahuatl are reproduced from a microfilm secured in 1938 by the School of American Research from the Biblioteca Medicea Laurenziana, Florence, Italy, of Sahagún's *General History of the Things of New Spain* manuscript. The illustrations, published here for the first time, are the work of sixteenth-century Aztec artists, and the Nahuatl paragraphs demonstrate the penmanship of Sahagún's native scribes. Permission to reproduce this material was granted by the Biblioteca Medicea Laurenziana and the School of American Research in Santa Fe, New Mexico.

ABOUT THE MAPS: The two maps and their embellishments were drawn by Arthur J. O. Anderson, and are based on details from Sahagún's original manuscript and other native codices.

University of Utah Press
Salt Lake City, Utah 84112

CONTENTS

INTRODUCTION

If the present native Indian account was set down in writing in about 1555, as seems likely, it was recorded just twenty-four or twenty-five years after the conquest of the Aztec nation had occurred. Though written record of the defeat of the Aztecs had taken form in song as early as 1524 and in narrative as early as 1528, the present account is the longest early, consistent, and fairly broad one that we have.

We owe its existence to the tireless effort and search for knowledge about the Aztecs of Fray Bernardino de Sahagún, one of the first Franciscan missionaries in Mexico. Casting about for means of complete and enduring conversion of the natives, he conceived and developed the theory that the priests would be more certain of success in their work if they knew, first, the total way of the Indians' former life they were changing and, second, the language the natives spoke — which the missionaries would have to master thoroughly. So, with the help of natives by the 1540s educated to reproduce in our alphabet the sounds of their own language and to read, write, and speak Spanish (and also Latin), Sahagún adopted the method of visiting and studying ancient native life in three centers in or about what is now Mexico City and, in each, winning the confidence of a dozen or so old men with experience and long memories, who answered his questions using the old picture writing, which the old men explained to the young literate Indians, who then wrote down the information in Aztec. The thirty or so years that followed were largely devoted to going over, comparing, arranging and rearranging, and writing up in final form what Sahagún and his young men had learned from the old ones who had been alive and young before the Spaniards came to conquer them.

Four hundred years ago Sahagún devised the method we have described. It is much like what a scientist of today would do as a matter of course.

Sahagún asked mainly about the Indians' old pre-Christian religious beliefs and rites, but he also got a descriptive picture so complete that his work is really a kind of encyclopaedia, in twelve "Books," which we call the *General History of the Things of New Spain*. In its most complete manuscript it is known as the *Florentine Codex*, because the original is in Florence, Italy. A bilingual work — a column in the Aztec language and another in Spanish

ix

on each page — it is, from the Spanish version, the ultimate source of all the Spanish Sahagún *Historias* printed since 1829. The Spanish column is not an exact translation of the native Nahuatl or Aztec; often it is rather a paraphrase. Translations of parts of the Aztec have appeared during the last eighty years or so, but ours of the entire *Florentine Codex* native text, concluded in 1969, is the first complete such translation of the work as a whole.

In some ways, one of the most original ideas Sahagún had in his work was getting from old Aztecs who were there before 1519–1521 their own account of the coming of the Spaniards and of defeat at their hands. This story forms the twelfth and last Book of the *General History*. Though it is a part of the total publication of the *General History* or *Florentine Codex*, it is so vivid and moving a story that we have reworked our English translation for this edition. The language is modernized but without changing the flavor of the native account; the original forty-one chapters have been reorganized into nine without altering the order of telling the events; there has been some condensing of wordy or repetitious passages; the point of view has been made more definitely Aztec. Nothing has been left out of the narrative. We have omitted our notes to the *Florentine Codex*; on controversial matters of translation the reader may refer to our original edition, which includes the Aztec text and is fully annotated. In this edition we include only a few explanatory notes, generally avoiding the controversies. Sahagún's account breaks off in the middle of a conference between Cortés and captured Indian leaders; we have not attempted to complete it, though we have added a brief epilogue.

*   *   *

We cannot and do not claim that the Aztec account is accurate and dispassionate. It is, naturally, incomplete and partisan. It is less complete than Bernal Díaz del Castillo's account and the one that emerges from Hernán Cortés's dispatches to King Charles I of Spain (who was also the Emperor Charles V of the Holy Roman Empire of those days); but in our judgment the Aztec account is no more partisan than either Bernal Díaz's or Hernán Cortés's. It is a sad story — one which, we think, shows remarkably little resentment toward Cortés and his followers. Wars are won or lost; the Aztecs lost this one — one which they never really had a chance of winning.

As to the accuracy of the account, the main features of the long struggle are there as the Aztecs saw (or were told) and remembered them. So, for example, a great deal of what happened is telescoped or told as if with a foreshortened perspective. The story begins with Grijalva's expedition, leaving out Francisco Hernández's earlier one; the details of Cortés's landing are omitted (we have the impression of there being only one ship in his fleet), and it took much longer than indicated in the Aztec account for Cortés and his men to reach the Valley of Mexico; the fighting against the Otomí settlements under Tlaxcallan rule took weeks and was more than a matter of "the batting of an eyelash"; Moctezuma was not captured immediately upon the entrance of the Spaniards into Tenochtitlan but about a week later. The reader can compare standard texts or, besides the Cortés and Bernal Díaz versions, other accounts of the time or a little later. Those by Aguilar, Cervantes de Salazar, López de Gómara, the anonymous conqueror, and others are one-sided but present a military situation more in keeping with our understanding of it than the native accounts are.

For reference and comparison we include our rough chronology of the events of the conquest followed by a summary of the only consistent chronology to be found in our native account.

CHART 1

ROUGH CHRONOLOGY OF THE CONQUEST OF MEXICO
ACCORDING TO STANDARD SOURCES

February, 1519	Departure of Cortés from Cuba.
	Arrival in Cozumel; finding of Aguilar.
March	Arrival in Tabasco; finding of Marina.
April	Arrival in Veracruz.
May	Founding of the Villa Rica de Veracruz.
	Burning of Cortés's ships.
August	Start of the march inland.
	Winning over of Cempoalla.*
September	Arrival in Tlaxcallan territory.
	Series of military engagements; winning over of Tlaxcalla.
October	Moctezuma's invitation to Cortés to proceed to Tenochtitlan.
	The Cholula massacre.
November	Moctezuma's reception of Cortés in Tenochtitlan.
	Cortés's capture of Moctezuma.
April, 1520	Cortés's defeat of Pánfilo de Narváez.
	Alvarado's massacre of Mexicans in Tenochtitlan.
	Death of Moctezuma.

xi

June	Flight of Spaniards from Tenochtitlan.
	Retreat of Spaniards to Tlaxcalla.
	Smallpox epidemic.
Fall of 1520	Capture of Texcoco (base for assembling Cortés's brigantines.)
December	Cortés's preparations for attack.
December, 1520– May, 1521	Encirclement of Mexico (capture of towns about the lake.)
May, 1521	Start of siege of Mexico.
August	End of siege of Mexico.

* The pronunciation of Aztec words: Generally speaking, vowels are pronounced as in Spanish or Italian: *a* as in fAther; *e* as in bEt; *i* as in machIne; *o* as in bOre; *u* as in rUle.

Consonants are generally pronounced as in English or as we are accustomed to hearing them in Spanish or Italian. Note, however, some special cases: *h*: usually not pronounced; *ll*: as in English or Italian (not as in Spanish); *qu*: like *k* before *e* and *i* (quemitl: kemitl; quilitl: kilitl), otherwise *kw* (qualli: kwalli); *u*: sometimes used consonantally, like English *w*, as in the name Coyoueuetzin (Coyowewetzin); *x*: like English *sh* (Xoloco: Sholoco); *z*: like English *ss* (Tizoc: Tissoc).

The stress is almost invariably on the next-to-last syllable.

CHART 2

Aztec Chronology of the Conquest as Recorded in Chapter V,
Page 61, and Chapter VI, Pages 63-64,
of the present account

Note: The solar year was divided into eighteen twenty-day periods (360 days) plus five final "empty" days (making 365 days). Corresponding Christian calendar dates are based on Alfonso Caso's calculations, which are generally accepted, though we begin the year with Atl caualo, as Sahagún does, while Caso begins with Izcalli. The Aztec text accidentally omits three of the month names, and occasional discrepancies may be noted.

Quecholli (Nov. 1–20, 1519). Entrance of the Spaniards on ceremonial calendar day One Wind, "the day before the tenth of the month Quecholli." (The year was named One Reed.)

Panquetzaliztli (Nov. 21–Dec. 10, 1519)

Atemoztli (Dec. 11–30, 1519)

Tititl (Dec. 31, 1519–Jan. 19, 1520)

Izcalli (Jan. 20–Feb. 8, 1520)

Nemontemi (the five "empty" days, Feb. 9–13, 1520)

Atl caualo (Feb. 14–Mar. 4, 1520)

Tlacaxipeualiztli (Mar. 5–24, 1520)

Tozoztontli (Mar. 25–Apr. 13, 1520)

Uei tozoztli (Apr. 14–May 3, 1520)

Toxcatl (May 4–23, 1520). Massacre in Tenochtitlan.

Etzalqualiztli (May 24–June 12, 1520)

Tecuilhuitontli (June 13–July 2, 1520). Escape of the Spaniards. "If all the days completed are added up, they come to two hundred and thirty-five. They had been our friends one hundred and ninety-five days. They had been our enemies forty days."

Uei tecuilhuitl (July 3–22, 1520). Resumption of the observance of the ancient feast days of this month noted.

Tlaxochimaco (July 23–Aug. 11, 1520)

Xocotl uetzi (Aug. 12–31, 1520)

Ochpaniztli (Sept. 1–20, 1520)

Teotl eco (Sept. 21–Oct. 10, 1520) ⎫ Beginning of smallpox epidemic

Tepeilhuitl (Oct. 11–30, 1520) ⎭ in one of these two months.

Quecholli (Oct. 31–Nov. 19, 1520)

Panquetzaliztli (Nov. 20–Dec. 9, 1520). "The pestilence . . . was diminishing."

Atemoztli (Dec. 10–29, 1520)

Tititl (Dec. 30, 1520–Jan. 18, 1521)

Izcalli (Jan. 19–Feb. 7, 1521). The Spaniards "were approaching from the direction of Quauhtitlan."

Nemontemi (Feb. 8–12, 1521)

Atl caualo (Feb. 13–Mar. 4, 1521)

Tlacaxipeualiztli (Mar. 5–24, 1521)

Tozoztontli (Mar. 25–Apr. 13, 1521)

Uei tozoztli (Apr. 14–May 3, 1521)

Toxcatl (May 4–23, 1521). The Spaniards "held consultations, councils of war, about us."

Etzalqualiztli (May 24–June 12, 1521)

Tecuilhuitontli (June 13–July 2, 1521). It was "a year since the Spaniards had died in the Tolteca canal."

*　　*　　*

Year Three House, ceremonial calendar day One Serpent: ". . . the shields were laid down. . . ."

Neither the natives of the New World nor the conquering Spaniards had any understanding of each other's civilization — from the ideals that motivated peaceful and gracious acts down to practical matters such as why and how war was waged.

As to warring: the Spaniards, fresh from successfully unifying Spain on the defeat and expulsion of the Moslems in 1492, were seasoned fighters accounted as the best-trained practitioners of the art of war as it was waged in the fifteenth and sixteenth centuries. Armies, with armor, bows, crossbows, spears, halberds, swords, arquebuses, primitive cannon, horses, and so on, contended against each other more or less as they do now to win battles, territory, booty, renown, and eventual material reward for king, leader, and humbler participant. A great many conquistadores, members of a usually penurious minor nobility, had come to the New World and continued to arrive — young, active, ambitious to carve out for themselves high status with wealth and equality with or a degree of independence from upper Spanish officialdom, whether in the New World or the Old. Practices had been established whereby new lands and their populations were claimed for the king following legal formulae; records were kept of the expedition's moves and acts; a priest or priests usually formed an important part of the personnel.

Above all, the conquistador, like the European of his and our times, fought to win the battle, the campaign, the war, and the benefits he expected from victory. There still remained from medieval times, however, vestiges of chivalrous ideals, which in some ways can interestingly be compared with the Aztec ideal of a warrior's life.

To a degree such may also have been Mesoamerican goals in fighting. Battles, campaigns, wars were won and benefits gained. But at the time of the conquest, and perhaps for centuries before, the war situation was highly colored, often completely dominated, by each warrior's need personally to take live prisoners to enhance his status and to serve the gods. This matter will be touched upon later; here we need only draw attention to the many times the taking of captives is stressed in the native account. Indeed, the taking of prisoners mitigated many a defeat.

* * *

Some two or three hundred years after the collapse, about a thousand years ago, of a "Classic" period of developing civilization which from our perspective looks like a long, relatively peaceful growth of Mesoamerican centers under what appears to have been priestly rule, control of events in central Mexico was taken over by much more warlike newcomers. These were the Toltecs, fighters and expansionists despite their being associated with the reputedly peace-loving Quetzalcoatl. They disappeared in their turn and, beginning about A.D. 1200, other barbarous and varied strangers from northerly parts took their place. These were the Chichimecs — the name could mean "dog people" — among the latest of whom were the Aztecs. After humiliations and vicissitudes, this tribe settled a cluster of unattractive islands in a corner of the connected lakes then covering most of the Valley of Mexico. Traditions set this event at about the year 1325. By the middle 1400s they had become the dominant population (allied with the people of Texcoco and Tlacopan, now Tacuba) not only in central Mexico but in extensive regions to the east, south, and west.

By a process of taking over the existing highly developed civilization and adapting it where necessary to their specialties, they represented a way of life in some ways more complex and in some ways simpler than that of their predecessors. It was basically agricultural and at the same time extremely warlike. In the island capital, Tenochtitlan, now Mexico City, the main pyramid in the central temple area was topped by two temples, one dedicated to Tlaloc, the rain and vegetation god, the other to Huitzilopochtli, the sun-war god. Of the two, the war god's temple was taller; and, in fact, the status of the successful warrior was infinitely higher than that of the agricultural worker (essential though he was) and indeed superior to all other callings except possibly the priesthood — though priest and warrior were so often the same as to make distinctions and generalizations uneasy. The social system provided, in any case, a strictly maintained class system — roughly noble and common, with a lower level, or levels, that ranged from a generally not too onerous form of serfdom to a generally mild form of slavery. This system was complicated by the recognition of many gradations of status. For instance: Traveling merchants, largely because so useful in warring preparations and aftermath, were almost nobility *per se*, and certain craftsmen like metalsmiths, lapidaries, and feather artists were almost equal in status to the merchants. Besides, such factors as success in war, the priesthood, long-distance trade, and craftsmanship could and did constantly provide the upper classes with new members, stringent though the rules of society were.

War can be said to have kept the Aztec system going. Religion required it: The hearts and blood of sacrificial victims nourished the sun and other gods and kept the universe in working order. Social status required it: The successful individual thus rose in rank and importance, and continued success maintained the status for him and for his sons if they too could measure up. The success, expansion, and wealth of the state required it as well. The relationships between religious beliefs and practices, warriors' success, and one's position in society were indissoluble. The warrior must bring home living captives for the sacrifices; and he joined the sun in the most magnificent of heavens if he died in war or on the sacrificial stone. Because the normal glorious end for all men was death in battle or on the sacrificial stone, women had their chance: as sacrifices or, if dead in childbirth, regarded as warriors killed in battle in the act of taking a captive for the god.

We emphasize these aspects of Aztec life because we think the Aztecs did so too, and because their way of thinking and acting in war was among the reasons they lost to the Spaniards when theoretically, though perhaps only temporarily, they could have won. There were other reasons for their defeat, of course, the importance of which is hard to assess. One was the general expectation, held more widely than just by the Aztecs and their allies, that Quetzalcoatl (godly ruler of the Toltecs), who had been forced to leave, sailing eastward in a boat formed of interlaced snakes, would eventually return to claim his due. He had so stated as he departed. How, therefore, should Cortés and his Spaniards, who in many ways seemed to fulfill that promise, be treated? This was a dilemma confronting the Aztecs. And there were the practical reasons: Spanish armor, horses, wheels, gunpowder, crossbows, boats, and so on. But perhaps it was as much as anything the difference in playing the game that lost it for the Aztecs: the Spanish attacks without elaborate warnings and their tactics and strategy aimed at winning the engagement and ultimately the war and complete control of all the population versus the Aztec tactics and strategy based primarily on the taking of live captives.

There was more than war and agriculture to the life of the Aztecs. They are known for the massive architecture of their public buildings and their equally massive sculpture and sculptural effects, but they were just as capable in the arts requiring great skill on a reduced scale — pottery, lapidary work, metal work, feather art, etc. There were many beautiful aspects to their religious, philosophical, and literary achievements that we often forget to take into account. These were perpetuated largely by word of mouth from one generation to the next; but with their system of pictorial writing (which had its awkward features) they could also keep records covering a wide variety of subject matter. To these is related a lively sense of time-measurement by means of (1) an eighteen-month system of twenty days each plus five "empty" days, (2) a ceremonial two-hundred-and-sixty-day calendar resulting from the mathematical combination of thirteen numbers with twenty day signs, and (3) the interplay of these two calendar systems by which the starting points

xvi

of each corresponded in such a way that every fifty-two years the people completed a full "bundle" of years and started a new fifty-two-year cycle. Though many of their treatments of disease depended upon certain services to the gods and were thought to hang upon the gods' whims, many cures were soundly based on knowledge of the properties of herbs, knowledge of anatomy, and proven surgical practices. These last the Spaniards appreciated often enough after an engagement with the Aztecs. Though our knowledge of their housing, at least for the middle to upper classes, is limited — that of the commoner who worked the fields probably remained little changed up to modern times — it is quite possible that the noble, merchant, commoner, and even the inferior classes on the whole may have lived better and more comfortably than did their contemporary counterparts in Europe.

But there are many sources of information on Aztec civilization in general to which the reader may refer for an abundance of detailed information. One of the most stirring descriptions of Tenochtitlan or Mexico City just before its destruction forms a part of Cortés's second dispatch to Charles V. The following is a broad translation of Cortés's remarks. Starting with the relatively flat Valley of Mexico, he says:

> . . . in said plain are two lakes which almost fill it. . . . One of these two lakes is of fresh water and the other, which is larger, is salty. . . . From one lake to another and among the cities and other settlements which are about said lakes, communication is by means of canoes, . . . with no need of going overland. . . .
>
> This great city of [Tenochtitlan] is built in the salt lake. From any direction one may wish to enter, the city is two leagues from the shore. It has four entrances, each an artificial causeway two short lance lengths in width. The city is about the same size as Seville or Córdoba. Its main streets are very wide and straight. Some of these and all the others are half solid roadway and half canal for canoe traffic. All the streets are open at intervals where canals join. But in all these gaps, some of which are very broad, there are bridges made of great, wide, shaped, close-set beams. On many of these ten horses could walk abreast. . . .
>
> This city has many open squares where markets and trade are continuous. One of the plazas is twice the size of that of Salamanca; it has a portico all the way around, where daily more than sixty thousand people meet to buy and sell all kinds of goods. . . . Each sort is sold in its own street, with no other kind of goods intruding, and in all of this the people maintain excellent order. They sell everything by the piece or by measure, . . . I have never seen them sell anything by weight. In this great plaza there is a large building like a court house where always are seated perhaps

ten or twelve judges who try all the market place cases and questions which arise there and have the guilty punished. . . .

In this city's various quarters there are many temple groups or buildings for their idols, of beautiful architecture. In the main areas the priestly cult personnel reside permanently. For them, besides the buildings for the idols, good quarters are provided. All these priests dress in black, and they never cut nor comb their hair from the time they enter the priesthood until they leave it. All the sons of the principal people, lords as well as respected commoners, remain in these religious establishments, costumed like the priests, from the age of seven or eight until they are released in order to marry — more usually the older ones who are to inherit property than the others. . . . Among the temple areas there is one, the greatest, which cannot be adequately described in words. It is so large that in its precincts, which are surrounded by a wall, there could well lie a settlement of five hundred. Inside this area, about its edges, are fine buildings with large halls and corridors where lodge the priests who are there. There are at least forty pyramids, very tall and well made; the largest has fifty steps leading up to the main body of the pyramid. The principal pyramid is taller than the Seville cathedral's tower. The stone masonry and the woodwork are equally good; they could nowhere be bettered. All the stone work inside the temples where they keep the idols is sculptured and plaster-roofed, and the woodwork is all carved in relief and painted with pictures of monsters and other figures and designs. All these pyramids are burial places for the lords, and each temple is dedicated to its idol, which they worship.

There are three halls within this great temple area in which are the principal idols, of marvelous size, height, and varied design, whether sculptured in stone or in wood. Within these halls are other chapels with very small entrances; they are completely dark. In them are only the priests, though not all of them, and the images of the gods, though, as I have said, there are many outside. . . .

There are many beautiful, large houses in this city, . . . for all the lords of the land, Moctezuma's vassals, have their houses here and reside in them part of the year. Besides, there are many rich citizens who also have very good houses. All of them have, besides good, large quarters, very fine flower gardens of various sorts, in houses of both high and low quality.

Along one of the causeways to the city are two conduits made of mortar, each two paces wide and almost two yards high. Through one of them flows a stream of good, fresh water as thick as a man's body, which reaches the center of the city. Everyone uses and drinks it. The other conduit is empty; when they wish to clean the one, they let the other take the flow of water. The water has to cross the city's salty canals over the bridges; it passes across in open conduits as thick as a bull and as long as the bridge. Thus the whole city is supplied. They deliver the water for sale along all the streets in canoes; when a canoe comes under a bridge where

xviii

there is an open conduit, men fill the canoes from above and are paid for their work.

At each entrance to the city and at every place where canoes unload, where most of the food reaches the city, there are huts for guards who keep a certain proportion of all that enters. . . .

In all the markets and public places . . . there daily gather many workers and experts in all the crafts awaiting anyone who may hire them by the day. In dress and activities the people of this city exhibit higher quality than those of other provinces and cities, for as the ruler Moctezuma has always been in the city with all his vassal lords, it has accumulated higher quality and polish in all things. . . . The people's activities and behavior are on almost as high a level as in Spain, and as well organized and orderly. Considering that these people are barbarous, lacking knowledge of God and communication with other civilized nations, it is remarkable to see all that they have. . . .

Such was Cortés's eye-witness impression in 1519 of the city he was to destroy almost two years later. Now follows the Aztec account of the calamity.

The War of Conquest
How It Was Waged Here in Mexico

TO THE READER

by

Fr. Bernardino de Sahagún

ALTHOUGH many have written of the conquest of this New Spain in Spanish, according to the account of those who conquered it, I desired to write it in the Mexican language, not so much to derive certain truths from the account of the very Indians who took part in the conquest, as to record the language of warfare and the weapons which the natives use in it, in order that the terms and proper modes of expression for speaking on this subject in the Mexican language can be derived therefrom. To this may be added that those who were conquered knew and gave an account of many things which transpired among them during the war, of which those who conquered them were unaware. For these reasons, it seems to me, to have written this history, which was written at a time when those who took part in the very conquest were alive, has not been a superfluous task. And those who gave this account [were] principal persons of good judgment, and it is believed they told all the truth.

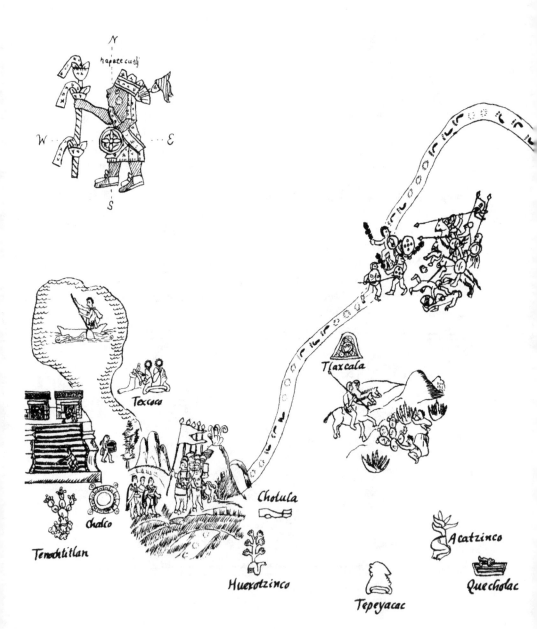

N

napatecutli

W   E

S

Texcoco

Tlaxcala

Chalco

Cholula

Tenochtitlan

Acatzinco

Huexotzinco

Quecholac

Tepeyacac

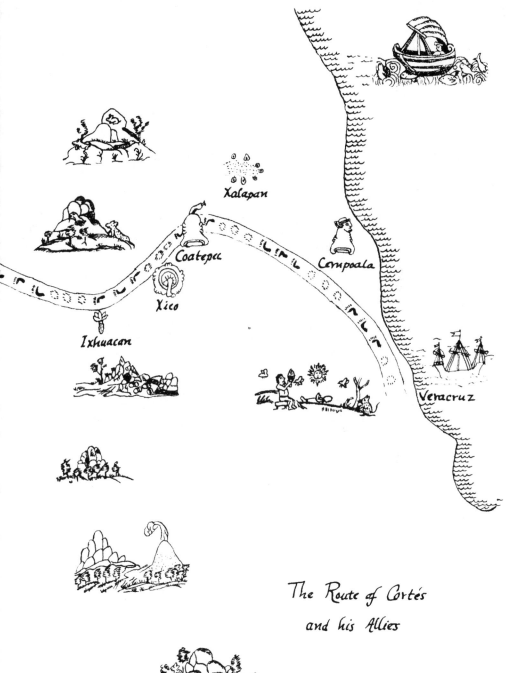

Xalapan

Coatepec

Xico

Ixhuacan

Cempoala

Veracruz

The Route of Cortés
and his Allies

I

PRELUDE OF EVIL SIGNS

EVEN BEFORE the Spaniards landed in New Spain, omens foretold their coming. These began ten years before the Conquest.

First, every night there arose a sign like a tongue of fire, like a flame. Pointed and wide-based, it pierced the heavens to their mid-point, their very heart. All night, off to the east, it looked as if day had dawned. Then the sun arose and destroyed it.

This went on for a year — the year of Twelve House.[1]

Every time the sign appeared, there was shouting. The men yelled, striking the palms of their hands against their mouths.[2] They were afraid and could think of nothing else.

Next, quite of its own accord, at Itepeyoc, at Tlacateccan,[3] Uitzilopochtli's temple burst into flame. No man could have set it; it burned of itself. When first seen, its squared, wooden columns were on fire and puffs of flame exploded from it as the flames ate all the beams. There was a great outcry. Priests called, "Hurry, Mexicans! Fight the

There arose a sign like a tongue of fire.

Quite of its own accord, Uitzilopochtli's temple burst into flame.

---

[1] The names of the Aztec years were derived from a series of four year signs — Rabbit, Reed, Flint, and House — combined with a series of thirteen numbers, e.g., One Rabbit, Two Reed, Three Flint, Four House, Five Rabbit, etc. A cycle of fifty-two years resulted from combining the two series.

[2] This would produce an ululant, pulsating shriek. It seems to have been a common war cry.

[3] Itepeyoc was that part of the temple of Uitzilopochtli where his image was formed; Tlacateccan is synonymous with Tlacatecco, alternative name for the temple of Uitzilopochtli.

7

fire! Bring water!" But the more water they threw on, the higher the flames flared. Nothing helped. It all went up.

Then lightning struck the straw roof of Tzonmulco, the temple of the old fire god Xiuhtecutli. This happened during not a storm but a mere sprinkle with just a summer flash—not even a thunder clap. Hence it was a sign of evil.

Other signs followed. In full light one late afternoon a comet appeared, bursting into three heads. It hurtled from west to east scattering sparks like glowing coals and leaving a long tail. Men raised a great shout when they saw it, for there was a rattling sound; a sound as of shell rattles spread everywhere.

Then the waters of the lake boiled up, crackling, and welled upward, far enough to melt adobes and tumble houses on the island. The day was still; there was no wind.

And often, in the dark of the night, a woman was heard moving, weeping. She would pace about wailing, "My dear children, we have to go! Where can I take you?"

One morning — this was the seventh sign — the fishing-folk while snaring birds came upon one like a brown crane with features so ominous that they took it where Moctezuma was meditating in the Tlillan calmecatl.[4] Its crest was like a round mirror pierced in the center like one a god might use to look into the future. There Moctezuma peered, to see the heavens — the stars — the fire drill constellation. He was first startled, and then terrified, as he saw, a little beyond, what looked like fighting men

---

[4] Tlillan calmecatl was the black dwelling place of the priests.

Lightning struck the straw roof of Tzonmulco.

In full light a comet appeared.

A woman was heard moving, weeping.

Its crest was like a round mirror pierced in the center.

Thistle people -- single-bodied but two-headed — appeared.

massed, like conquerors in war array, riding the backs of deer. He summoned his wise men. "Can you tell me," he asked, "what is the meaning of what I have just seen there, like fighters marching massed?" But when they looked, they saw nothing. They could give him no answer.

Finally, thistle-people—single-bodied but two-headed -- often appeared. As often as anybody found one he took it to Moctezuma. As soon as he looked at one it would vanish.

Prodigies like these foretold the coming of the Spaniards years before they came.

II

THE LANDINGS

ONLY ONE vessel came, to begin with.[1] As the Spaniards sailed along the shore, they were reported. The high steward of Cuetlaxtlan, a man called Pinotl, went there himself to see. He took four witnesses: Yaotzin, steward of Mictlanquauhtla; Teocinyaotl, steward of Teocinyocan; and Cuitlalpitoc and Tentlil, who were underlings, guides. They went to look, to spy, to size the strangers up. But as a precaution they decided to offer them a gift of precious capes,[2] the sort reserved exclusively for Moctezuma, his prerogative alone, which none else might wear.

Pinotl had said, "Our lives would be worth little if we were to deceive Moctezuma. Therefore we must go and look, so that we can truthfully report to him." So they got sea coast people to paddle them out to the Spaniards. Drawing near enough to see them and be seen, they went through motions at the prows of the boats as if kissing

the earth. For they thought Quetzalcoatl must at last have come back in that vessel.[3]

The Spaniards, through interpreters, called out to them, "Who are you? Where from?"

"We have come from Mexico."

"Are you indeed Mexicans? What then is the name of your ruler?"

"O lords," the Mexicans answered, "his name is Moctezuma."

And in his name they gave the Spaniards the gifts they had carried out — precious capes with the sign of the sun, with blue knotted work, with figures of jars, with eagle down, with snake heads, with Quetzalcoatl's wind jewel, with the turkey blood design, with the whirlpool or the smoking mirror design.... All these they gave the Spaniards. In return they accepted necklaces of blue and yellow which looked like amber, and they wondered greatly at these beads.

Then the Spaniards dismissed them. "Go," they said. "We go back to Spain but shall soon return."

So the Spaniards sailed away whence they came, the Mexican officials waiting ashore until they had left and then setting forth to

[1] This refers to Juan de Grijalva's arrival at Isla de los Sacrificios, an island in the present-day Veracruz. He arrived in 1518.

[2] These were unique because of materials used, ornamentation (feathers, fringes, etc.), color, design woven in, etc.

[3] According to one account, that in the *Anales de Cuauhtitlan*, Quetzalcoatl, upon reaching the sea shore in his flight from Tula, cast himself into a funeral pyre, his heart becoming the morning star. The account Sahagún gives in the third Book of the *General History* is that he sailed eastward on a raft of intertwined snakes. It was assured he would return from the east to resume his rule.

Mexico. Day and night they sped inland to warn Moctezuma, to inform him of the truth of what had happened and of the exchange of gifts.

Arriving, they said, "O lord, O noble young man, be merciful to us. Hear what we have seen and what we have done there where your old men watch the sea for you.

"We went out into the water to see our lords the gods. We gave them all your capes which we had with us. Here are the lordly things they gave us.

"They said to us, 'If you came from Mexico, then give these to the ruler Moctezuma, so that he may recognize us when we return.'"

So they gave Moctezuma a complete account of their meeting and speaking with the Spaniards in the sea.

Moctezuma answered, "You have traveled far; you are tired. Rest. What you have shown me is to remain secret. Let no one speak of it. This has been between you and me only."

He then commanded Pinotl and the others, "See that the shoreline is constantly watched everywhere — at Nauhtlan, at Toztlan, at Mictlanquauhtla; wherever the strangers may land."

And the stewards then left to see that the command was carried out.

Meanwhile Moctezuma called together his most trusted lords, his deputy Tlilpoton-qui, the high warriors Quappiaztzin and Quetzalaztatzin, and the high judge Ecatenpatiltzin, to inform them, and he showed them the beads brought by the stewards.

"Now that we have gaped over these fine turquoises," he said, "let them be well guarded. Let the keepers watch them well, for if they lose even one piece, I shall take from them their houses, their children, their wives."

Time passed, so that the year of Twelve Flint Knife was followed by its companion, Thirteen Rabbit. And when the year Thirteen Rabbit was about to complete its term,[4] then Spaniards again sailed along the shoreline. They landed. The stewards again sped to inform Moctezuma. And Moctezuma acted; for he thought, as everyone else did, that it surely was Quetzalcoatl who had returned, as he had said he would when he set out eastward long ago, to resume the rulership from which he had been driven.

Moctezuma then chose five to represent him and go to meet the Spaniards. He commissioned the lordly priest Yoalli ichan with personages from Tepoztlan, from Tizatlan, from Ueuetlan, from Ueicamecatlan. He said to them, "Come, you jaguar warriors![5] We are told that our lord Quetzalcoatl has finally landed. Go to meet him; listen to him carefully; repeat to me faithfully what he says. These are the gifts you will take him."

---

[4] The year Thirteen Rabbit ended January 24, 1519; the following year, One Reed, began January 25, 1519. Cortés arrived at the port of San Juan de Ulúa on Holy Thursday, 1519.

[5] The successful Aztec was almost invariably a successful warrior. If unusually so, various high ranks or orders (like "jaguar") were open to him.

The gifts were four complete sets of gods' array.[6]

The first array was that of Quetzalcoatl. It consisted of a snake mask in turquoise mosaic; a quetzal-feather, fan-shaped head ornament; a plaited jadeite neckband in which nestled a disc of gold; a shield with bands of gold, or of gold and seashells, crisscrossed, with quetzal feathers and a quetzal flag at its lower edge; a turquoise-mosaic-backed mirror with quetzal feathers for the small of the back; more neckbands of jadeite and golden shells; a turquoise spear thrower, all turquoise with a snake-head ornament; and black "obsidian" sandals.

Second, they assembled an array suitable for the god Tezcatlipoca — a gold-starred feather headdress; earplugs like golden shells; a necklace of seashells; a breast ornament, itself and its fringe sewn with seashells; a sleeveless jerkin with design, eyeleted border, and feathered edging; a mosaic mirror for the small of the back; golden shells to ornament the calves of the legs; and white sandals.

Third was the god Tlaloc's array. His characteristic heron feather headdress was made entirely of quetzal feathers, under a band of shells crossing another of gold. He had snake-head earplugs of jadeite; a sleeveless jerkin with a design in jadeite; a neck ornament consisting of plaited jadeite and a disc of gold; a mirror for the small of the back; rattles; a cape with an edging of red rings; golden shell-like ornaments for the

ankles; and a turquoise mosaic staff designed like a snake.

Finally there was again Quetzalcoatl's finery.[7] It consisted of a peaked jaguar skin cap with pheasant plumes and, at its tip, a large jadeite stone; earplugs of turquoise mosaic with pendant golden seashells; a plaited jadeite neckband set off by a golden disc; a red-bordered cape; golden shell ornaments for the ankles; a shield in which a golden circle was centered and from whose lower edge hung quetzal feathers and a banner; the wind god's curved, hooked staff sown with white jadeite stars; and white "foam" sandals.

These were some of the godly array entrusted to Moctezuma's emissaries. There were other gifts of greeting — a golden, shell-shaped headdress with parrot feathers hanging; a golden conical cap; and so on. They filled baskets with these things and readied the wooden frames with which the burden-carriers carried loads upon their backs.

And Moctezuma told his five messengers, "Set out! Hurry! Give our prayers to the lord, the god Quetzalcoatl. Say to him, 'Your deputy governor Moctezuma has sent us; here are his gifts to you, for you have come to occupy Moctezuma's poor home here in Mexico.' "

The emissaries reached the shore; the seacoast people paddled them across to Xicalanco; then they again took to the boats,

---

[6] Since it was thought that gods had arrived, array no doubt considered appropriate to them was selected. Quetzalcoatl, Tezcatlipoca, and Tlaloc were among the very highest gods.

[7] Listing Quetzalcoatl's array twice may have been an error by Sahagún's informant or copyist.

heaping all the gifts about them. Taking off, they went toward the Spaniards' vessel.

Seeing them, the Spaniards through their interpreters called out, "Who are you? Where from?"

"We come from Mexico, over there."

"Maybe so, maybe not. You may just be fugitives. You may just pretend. You may be making fools of us," the Spaniards answered.

But when they were finally reassured, convinced, they caught the prows of the boats with iron poles, drew them up to the vessel, and let down a ladder. Then the Mexicans climbed up, carrying the godly array as a gift of greeting. Each one went through the motions of kissing the earth before Cortés.

"May it please the god to hear. His deputy governor, Moctezuma, who rules Mexico for him, prays to him and says, 'The god has traveled far; he is tired.'"

Then they dressed Cortés in the array of Quetzalcoatl: in the turquoise mosaic snake mask with the head fan of quetzal feathers and with the jadeite snake-head earplugs suspended from it; the sleeveless jerkin; the plaited jadeite neckband with the golden disc resting in its midst. On the small of his back they put the mirror; over his shoulders they bound the cape; about the calf of his leg they arranged the jadeite band with the golden shells. And on his arm they laid the shield with bands of gold and shells criss-crossed and with outspread quetzal feathers on the lower rim and a quetzal feather flag. In front of him they laid the black "obsidian" sandals.

The other three sets of godly array they arranged in order before him.

The Mexicans climbed up, carrying the godly array as a gift of greeting.

The Spaniards put irons about their necks; they fettered them.

14

Then they shot off the gun.

The Spaniards revived them with a drink of wine, and made them eat some food.

"Are these all your gifts of greeting, all your gifts for coming before one?" asked Cortés through interpreters, after all this had been done.

"These are all the things we have brought," they answered.

Then Cortés ordered them to be bound. The Spaniards put irons about their necks; they fettered them. Then they shot off the great lombard gun. At this, Moctezuma's emissaries fainted dead away — fell — knew no more, until the Spaniards sat each one up, revived them with a drink of wine, and made them eat some food.

After all this, Cortés said to them, "Listen. I have long since heard it said that Mexicans are very strong, very brave, great conquerors. One Mexican can put to flight, overcome, turn back even ten, even twenty of his foes. I now wish to be convinced; I wish to see you do it; I wish to test how strong, how powerful you are." Distributing leather shields, iron swords, iron lances, he continued, "And tomorrow, just before sunrise, we shall test each other; we shall fight each other on equal terms. Then we shall know who is better."

"But — may it please the lord to hear," they answered, "— the lord's deputy governor Moctezuma did not tell us to do that. He told us only to greet our lord on his behalf. If we were to do as our lord says, would Moctezuma not be angry? Would he not kill us?"

"No, for I will it to be. I wish to see, to test your abilities. For it is well known in Spain that you are very strong, very brave. Eat before dawn, as I shall. Prepare yourselves."

15

Cortés and the Spaniards then let them climb down to their boats.

They paddled off furiously, each one as hard as he could. Some paddled with their hands, so as to flee as fast as they could. They said to one another, "Warriors! All your strength, now! Row hard, lest something evil befall us!"

They sped first back to Xicalanco, resting there no more than to restore their strength quickly to press on to Tecpan tlayacac and then to Cuetlaxtlan.

The Cuetlaxtlan people said, "Rest here, if only for a day; gather your strength!"

But the emissaries answered, "No, we shall hurry on. We must warn Moctezuma; we must report what we saw, which has filled us with terror. The like has never been seen. Surely you would not expect that you be told of it before Moctezuma?"

So they hastened on, reaching Mexico deep in the night.

Meanwhile Moctezuma had been unable to rest, to sleep, to eat. He would speak to no one. He seemed to be in great torment. He sighed. He felt weak. He could enjoy nothing.

"What will happen now?" he kept asking. "Who will be lord as I have been until now? My heart is burning as if dipped in chili sauce. Where can we go, O lord?"

Then the five emissaries arrived. "Even if he is asleep," they told the guards, "wake him. Tell him that those he sent to the sea have returned."

But Moctezuma said, "I shall not hear them in this place. Have them go to the Coacalli building."[8] Further he commanded, "Have two captives covered with chalk."[9]

So the messengers went to the Coacalli, the house of snakes.

Moctezuma came later. In front of the messengers, the captives were killed — their hearts torn out, their blood sprinkled over

the messengers; for they had gone into great danger; they had looked into the very faces of the gods; they had even spoken to them.

After this they reported to Moctezuma all the wonders they had seen, and they showed him samples of the food the Spaniards ate.

---

[8] The Coacalli, the house of snakes, was a reception hall for visiting dignitaries and rulers, friendly or unfriendly to the Mexicans.

[9] Slaves and captives were covered with chalk and down feathers prior to sacrifice.

16

Moctezuma was shocked, terrified by what he heard. He was much puzzled by their food, but what made him almost faint away was the telling of how the great lombard gun, at the Spaniards' command, expelled the shot which thundered as it went off. The noise weakened one, dizzied one. Something like a stone came out of it in a shower of fire and sparks. The smoke was foul; it had a sickening, fetid smell. And the shot, which struck a mountain, knocked it to bits — dissolved it. It reduced a tree to sawdust -- the tree disappeared as if they had blown it away.

And as to their war gear, it was all iron. They were iron. Their head pieces were of iron. Their swords, their crossbows, their shields, their lances were of iron.[10]

The animals they rode -- they looked like deer -- were as high as roof tops.

They covered their bodies completely, all except their faces.

They were very white. Their eyes were like chalk. Their hair -- on some it was yellow, on some it was black. They wore long beards; they were yellow, too. And there were some black-skinned ones with kinky hair.

What they ate was like what Aztecs ate during periods of fasting: it was large, it was white, it was lighter than tortillas; it was spongy like the inside of corn stalks; it tasted as if it had been made of a flour of corn stalks; it was sweetish.

Their dogs were huge. Their ears were folded over; their jowls dragged; their eyes blazed yellow, fiery yellow. They were thin -- their ribs showed. They were big. They were restless, moving about panting, tongues hanging. They were spotted or varicolored like jaguars.[11]

When Moctezuma was told all this, he was terror-struck. He felt faint. His heart failed him.

As to their war gear, it was all of iron.

Moctezuma was told all this.

[10] The Aztecs saw little distinction between copper and iron. Iron was sometimes called "black copper."

[11] The dogs would have been mastiffs, hounds, probably other hunting dogs. They were evidently more terrifying in appearance than the native breeds of dog.

III

THE MARCH ON MEXICO

Nevertheless, Moctezuma then again sent emissaries, this time all the doers of evil he could gather—magicians, wizards, sorcerers, soothsayers. With them he sent the old men and the warriors necessary to requisition all the food the Spaniards would need, the turkeys, the eggs, the best white tortillas, everything necessary. The elders and fighting men were to care well for them.

Likewise he sent a contingent of captives, so that his men might be prepared in case the supposed gods required human blood to drink. And the emissaries indeed so thought, themselves. But the sacrifice nauseated the Spaniards. They shut their eyes tight; they shook their heads. For Moctezuma's men had soaked the food in blood before offering it to them; it revolted them, sickened them, so much did it reek of blood.

But Moctezuma had provided for this because, as he assumed them to be gods, he was worshipping them as gods. So were the Mexicans. They called these Spaniards "gods come from the heavens"; the Mexicans thought they were all gods, including the black ones, whom they called the dusky gods.

In due course the Spaniards ate; they had white tortillas, degrained corn, eggs, turkey, various kinds of sweet potato, manioc, avocado, acacia beans, and *jicama*, and ended with a choice of custard apple, mamey, sapota, plum, jobo, guava, *cuajilote*, *tejo-*

In due course the Spaniards ate.

cote, American cherry, blackberry, prickly pear, and *pitahaya*. Fodder was provided the deer — horses — which the Spaniards rode: stuff called *pipillo* and *tlachicaztli*.

As for the magicians, wizards, sorcerers, and soothsayers, Moctezuma had sent them just in case they might size up the Spaniards differently and be able to use their arts against them — cast a spell over them, blow them away, enchant them, throw stones at them, with wizards' words say an incantation over them — anything that might sicken them, kill them, or turn them back. They fulfilled their charge; they tried their skill on the Spaniards; but what they did had no effect whatsoever. They were powerless.

These men then returned to report to Moctezuma. "We are not as strong as they," was what they said as they described the Spaniards to him. "We are nothing compared to them."

Therefore Moctezuma strictly commanded the stewards, the lords, the elders, on pain of death to have at hand everything the Spaniards might need. Thus, when they had landed, as they progressed inland along the road, they were well provided for; they were treated with esteem. Completely in these emissaries' hands they started out with great ease. Everything was done for their comfort.

In Moctezuma's capital there was apprehension, sorrow, on this indication of the Spaniards' power. Shocked, terrified, Moctezuma himself wept in the distress he felt for his city.

Everyone was in terror; everyone was astounded, afflicted. Many huddled in groups, wept in foreboding for their own fates and those of their friends. Others, dejected, hung their heads. Some groups exchanged tearful greetings; others tried mutual encouragement. Fathers would run their hands over their small boys' hair and, smoothing it, say, "Woe, my beloved sons! How can what we fear be happening in your time?" Mothers, too: "My beloved sons, how can you live through what is in store for you?"

Then word came which pierced Moctezuma's heart: that a woman of our own race was bringing the Spaniards toward Mexico, was interpreting for them, a woman named Marina.[1] She came from Teticpac. The Spaniards had come upon her on the coast. It was at just this time that Moctezuma's emissaries began leaving the Spaniards alone. Those who had been procuring their food, who had been easing their way, just went off, just turned their backs on them.

And at about this time the Spaniards' questions about Moctezuma became urgent. "What kind of man is he? Young? Mature? Old? Advanced in years? Well preserved? Doddering? Is he white-headed?" To these

---

[1] On the banks of the Grijalva River, near the present town of Tabasco, the Spaniards fought and overcame the native forces. Numbered among the twenty native women given to the Spaniards was Marina, also known as La Malinche and later as Doña Marina. Born in the town of Painala, in the province of Coatzacoalcos, she had been sold to Mexican traders of Xicalanco and subsequently to Tabasco traders. Speaking Maya and Nahuatl, she quickly learned Spanish and became Cortés's interpreter.

Many huddled in groups, wept in foreboding.

A woman of our own race was bringing the Spaniards toward Mexico, a woman named Marina.

He turned the matter over, deciding to look for a likely cave.

questions of the gods — the Spaniards — the reply had been, "He is in his maturity. He is not fat; rather, he is slender, spare, thin."

But when Moctezuma learned that they inquired about him in this way, that they sought him, that these men, these gods, intended to look upon his face, his heart was afflicted with great apprehension. He tried to make plans to leave, to flee, to take himself hence, to hide himself, to seek a refuge from the gods. He turned the matter over in his mind for a long time, first deciding to look for a likely cave and then discussing the question with those to whom he could unburden himself, in whom he could confide. Among them were some who told him what they knew. "There are those," they said, "who know where the region of the dead is, the house of the sun, the realm of the god Tlaloc, the house of corn.[2] Decide where you would go."

It was to the house of corn that it was generally decided he should go. But he could not. There was no place where he could hide himself. No longer had he the time or energy. He could not bring to reality the words of the soothsayers who had promised him his refuge. They had only pretended, had only apparently taken vengeance on him for something.

Moctezuma could only wait for the Spaniards, could only show resolution. He

[2] Mictlan, the region of the dead, Tonatiuh ichan, the house of the sun, Tlalocan, the realm of the rain god Tlaloc, are abodes of the dead as determined by ones' deeds or the manner of his death. Cincalco, the house of corn, was believed to be a paradise to the west presided over by Huemac, the Toltec ruler. It was generally thought to be a cave in the vicinity of Chapultepec.

quieted, he controlled himself; he made himself submit to whatever was in store for him. So he left his proper dwelling, the great palace, so that the gods — the Spaniards — could occupy it, and moved to the palace he had originally occupied as a prince.

The Spaniards, pressing inland meanwhile to go through the city of Cempoalla, had with them a previously captured man known to have been a high warrior.[3] He was now interpreting for them and guiding them, since he knew the roads and could keep them on the right ones.

Thus they came to reach a place called Tecoac, held by people of the Otomí tribe subject to the city of Tlaxcalla. Here the men of Tecoac resisted; they came out with their weapons. But the Spaniards completely routed them. They trampled them down; they shot them down with their guns; they riddled them with the bolts of their crossbows. They annihilated them, not just a few but a great many.

When Tecoac perished, the news made the Tlaxcallans beside themselves with fear. They lost courage; they gave way to wonder, to terror, until they gathered themselves together and, at a meeting of the rulers, took counsel, weighed the news among themselves, and discussed what to do.

"How shall we act?" some asked. "Shall we meet with them?"

Others said, "The Otomís are great warriors, great fighters, yet the Spaniards thought nothing of them. They were as nothing. In no time, with but the batting of an eyelash, they annihilated our vassals."

"The only thing to do," advised still others, "is to submit to these men, to befriend them, to reconcile ourselves to them. Otherwise, sad would be the fate of the common folk."

This argument prevailed. The rulers of Tlaxcalla went to meet the Spaniards with food offerings of turkey, eggs, fine white tortillas — the tortillas of lords.

"You have tired yourselves, O our lords," they said.

The Spaniards asked, "Where is your home? Where are you from?"

"We are Tlaxcallans," they answered. "You have tired yourselves. You have come to your poor home, Quauhtlaxcalla."

The rulers of Tlaxcalla went to meet the Spaniards with food offerings.

---

[3] The native *tlacochcalcatl* (a high military official) had been taken in the earlier Grijalva expedition and Cortés had brought him along.

22

(Thus they called it—Eagle-Tlaxcalla—though in former times it had been known as Texcalla—Cragland—and its people were Texcallans.)

The Tlaxcallans led the Spaniards to the city, to their palace. They made much of them, gave them whatever they needed, waited upon them, and comforted them with their daughters.

The Spaniards, however, kept asking them "Where is Mexico? What is it like? Is it far?"

"From here it is not far," was the answer; "it is a matter of perhaps only three days' march. It is a very splendid place; the Mexicans are strong, brave, conquering people. You find them everywhere."

Now the Tlaxcallans had long been enemies of the people of Cholula. They disliked, hated, detested them; they would have nothing to do with them. Hoping to do them harm, they inflamed the Spaniards against them, saying, "They are very evil, these enemies of ours. Cholula is as powerful as Mexico. Cholula is friendly to Mexico."

Therefore the Spaniards at once went to Cholula, taking the Tlaxcallans and the Cempoallans with them all in war array. They arrived; they entered Cholula. Then there arose from the Spaniards a cry summoning all the noblemen, lords, war leaders, warriors, and common folk; and when they had crowded into the temple courtyard, then the Spaniards and their allies blocked the entrances and every exit.

There followed a butchery of stabbing, beating, killing of the unsuspecting Cholulans armed with no bows and arrows, protected by no shields, unable to contend against the Spaniards. So with no warning they were treacherously, deceitfully slain. The Tlaxcallans had induced the Spaniards to do this.

What had happened was reported quickly to Moctezuma: his messengers, who had just arrived, departed fleeing back to him. They did not remain long to learn all the details. The effect upon the people of Mexico, however, was immediate; they often rose in tumults, alarmed as by an earthquake, as if there were a constant reeling of the face of the earth. They were terrified.

After death came to Cholula, the Spaniards resumed their marching order to advance upon Mexico. They assembled in their accustomed groups, a multitude, raising a great dust. The iron of their lances and their halberds glistened from afar; the shimmer of their swords was as of a sinuous water course. Their iron breast and back pieces, their helmets clanked. Some came completely encased in iron — as if turned to iron, gleaming, resounding from afar. And ahead of them, preceding them, ran their dogs, panting, with foam continually dripping from their muzzles.

All this stunned the people, terrified them, filled them with fear, with dread.

23

It was at this juncture that Moctezuma sent a company of noblemen, with magicians, wizards, sorcerers, soothsayers, and priests to meet Cortés at Quauhtechcac, a point between the peaks of Iztac ciuatl and Popocatepetl.

The noblemen and court officials were led by Tziuacpopocatzin, to whom Moctezuma had entrusted a quantity of streamers of gold and of precious feathers, and necklaces of gold. These they were charged to give to Cortés and his men.

When they had delivered these gifts, the Spaniards appeared to be much gladdened, contented, delighted. They seized upon the gold as if they were monkeys, their faces gleaming. For clearly their thirst for gold was insatiable; they starved for it; they lusted for it; they wanted to stuff themselves with it as if they were pigs. So they went about fingering, taking up the streamers of gold, moving them back and forth, grabbing them to themselves, babbling, talking gibberish among themselves.

Then they noted Tziuacpopocatzin.

"Is that one Moctezuma?" they secretly asked the Tlaxcallans and Cempoallans who were watching among them.

"Not he, O our lords," they replied. "That one is Tziuacpopocatzin. Moctezuma merely deputized him."

So the Spaniards turned to him. "Are you Moctezuma?" they asked through the interpreters.

"I am your deputy governor," he said. "I am Moctezuma."

"Go away," they answered. "Why lie to us? What do you take us for? You cannot fool us. Moctezuma is in Mexico. He will

Moctezuma sent a company of noblemen, with magicians, wizards, sorcerers, soothsayers, and priests to meet Cortés.

The magicians, wizards, sorcerers, soothsayers, and priests went to inform Moctezuma.

24

not be able to hide from us. There is nowhere he can take refuge from us - - unless he is a bird. Can he fly? Can he burrow underground? We shall find him. We cannot fail to look into his face, to listen to the words which come from his lips."

Thus they held Moctezuma to scorn. Thus another meeting, another gift-giving, came to naught. Thus they could continue to despise Moctezuma. They at once pressed on, along the road direct to Mexico.

Meanwhile, the other part of the company sent by Moctezuma, the magicians, wizards, sorcerers, soothsayers, and priests, had come up, performed, and been equally unsuccessful. Nowhere in anything could they prevail; nowhere in anything could they make a show against the Spaniards.

On the road they met one who was as if drunk. As they came up to him, they could make nothing of him. He was arrayed like one from Chalco; he seemed to be drunk, inebriated; he was bound about the chest with eight grass ropes. He met them in front of the advancing Spanish column.

He flared up against them.

"What do you think you can still do with them?" he asked. "What more do you want? What does Moctezuma still hope to gain? Has he still not come to his senses? Is he beside himself with fear? He has sinned. He has deserted the people - - he has destroyed them. On his account their heads are broken, they are enveloped in the wrappings of the dead, they are made fun of, laughed at!"

When they had seen this prodigy and heard him speak, the magicians, wizards, sorcerers, soothsayers, and priests began to pay attention to him. But it was to no purpose. To no avail did they humbly pray to him. In vain they quickly set up his watching place, his earthen mound, his bed of straw. He ignored it all. What they had done, earthen mound and all, was for nothing.

He abused them. He said, "Why have you come here? It has been to no purpose. Nevermore will Mexico exist; it is already lost forever. Go away. It is there no longer. Turn around; look at what is to happen to Mexico — what is immediately in store!"

They turned to look. In the distance they could see all the temples, all the buildings of the administrative areas, all the higher educational buildings, all the houses as if in flames; and it looked as if already there were street fighting.

When the magicians, wizards, sorcerers, soothsayers and priests saw this, their hearts sank. They could no longer speak clearly; their words stuck in their throats.

They said to one another, "This is something we ought never to have looked at; it was a sight Moctezuma should have seen. For it is not just anybody who has accosted us; it is the youth himself, the god Tezcatlipoca!"

And when they realized who he was, the god vanished; they saw him no more.

No farther did the magicians, wizards, sorcerers, soothsayers, and priests go; right there they turned back; they went to inform Moctezuma. Eventually they joined Tziuac-popocatzin and those who had been of his company. And when they all arrived in Mexico, they reported the things that had happened, the things they had seen.

When he learned of these events, Moctezuma could only bow his head. He could only sit with head hanging. For a long time he sat dejected, not speaking aloud, as if he had lost hope.

He could only at last say to them, "What now, my warriors? We have come to the end. We have taken our medicine. Is there anywhere a mountain we can run away to and climb? But we are Mexicans; can the Mexican state maintain its accustomed glory? Evil is the fate of the poor old men and women, of the babes in arms. Where can they go? What is now to be done? Where can we go? We have now taken our medicine, whatever it is."

They could see all the temples, all the buildings as if in flames.

Moctezuma now had the road, the highway, blocked off in a last attempt to deflect the Spaniards from Mexico. The fork which led direct to Mexico he had planted with maguey, with century plant; he let them see the other road, which would take them to Texcoco. But they knew that it was only a

Moctezuma had the road blocked, planted with maguey.

false wall of maguey. They heeded it only to take it up; they kicked each plant aside; far away did they cast them.

There at Amaquemecan they slept. Then they continued; they marched direct along the road until they came to Cuitlauac, where next they slept. As they had already spoken to the rulers of Chalco, gaining their submission, there they likewise spoke to the rulers of the floating garden provinces, Xochimilco, Cuitlauac, and Mizquic. And the rulers of the floating gardens people also forthwith submitted to them.

Satisfied here, the Spaniards moved on and stopped at Itztapalapan, where once more they had the rulers brought together before them, those known as the Four Lords, lords of Itztapalapan, of Mexicatzinco, of Colhuacan, and of Uitzilopochco. Just as they had addressed the rulers of the floating gardens people, just so did they with these, making them respond in the same way. They, too, quietly and peacefully submitted.

And Moctezuma did nothing; he commanded no war, no strife against them. No one was to resist them in battle. He only commanded that they be cared for, that all be done for them.

And on this, Mexico lay as if stunned, silent. None went out of doors. Mothers kept their children in. The roads were clear — wide open, deserted, as if it were early morning. None even crossed the roads. People entered their houses there preoccupying themselves only with their afflictions. "So be it," the common folk said. "Let us be accursed. What more can be done? We are bound to die, we are already bound to perish. Yes, we can only await death."

The Spaniards once more had the rulers brought before them.

So now the host started to move, ready to converge on Mexico itself. The Spaniards put on their war gear; they girt on, bound on their battle dress. They arranged their horses; they disposed them in rows, placed them in line.

This was their order of march.

Four horsemen led; they made up the vanguard. They led, continuously turning about, continuously wheeling around, facing the onlooking people, peering hither and thither, watching every side, scanning all areas between the groups of houses, looking up to the roof terraces, their dogs scrambling ahead, sniffing each object, panting — continually panting.

27

Four horsemen led; they made up the vanguard.

They led, turning about, wheeling around, peering hither and thither.

Alone marched the bearer of the standard.

Alone marched the bearer of the standard. He carried it upon his shoulder, continually shaking it, making it circle and toss from side to side. It came continually stiffening in the wind, rising like a warrior, twisting and raising itself, twisting and filling itself out.

Then followed the bearers of iron swords, each sword flashing as the men went by. On their shoulders they bore shields — wooden shields, leather shields.

Next came a second file of horsemen each in a quilted cotton cuirass, each with leather shield and iron lance, each with an iron sword hanging at the horse's neck. Each had little bells; they all jingled by with a shattering jangle. The horses — they looked like deer — neighed and whinnied. They were all sweating; water fell from their bodies; large flecks of foam, like soap suds, flew from their mouths to the ground. Their hooves beat the dirt as they advanced, pounding, sounding like stones cast at us, piercing holes which appeared, each one separately, as each hoof lifted, as each hind leg and each foreleg stamped.

The third group consisted of men with iron crossbows resting on their arms. They went testing, wielding them as they marched, though some just rested them on their shoulders. At their sides or under their arms hung their quivers, each one filled, crammed with bolts. They had quilted cotton armor reaching to the knees — very thick armor, firmly sewn, exceedingly dense, thick, close-woven. The same quilted armor protected their heads, each one topped with precious feathers, all dividing and outspread.

Fourth rode more horsemen, arrayed like those just described.

Fifth marched a group of arquebusiers. Some bore their arquebuses on their shoulders, some carried them extended. When, later, they came to enter the great palace assigned the Spaniards, the ruler's great residence, they fired them, fired them repeatedly. Each one exploded, crackled, thundered as it discharged, as it disgorged its charge. Smoke spread, suffused, massed over, and darkened the ground. It spread all over, its fetid smell stupefying us, robbing us of our senses.

At the very last of this column, directing from behind, came the commander, Cortés, just like our highest warrior — the ruler, the director of battles. Surrounding him closely were those he knew, his brave warriors, his device-bearers, his attendants; those who were like our shorn-hair or our Otomí order of warriors; the intrepid ones; the main support, the soul, the foundation of the state.

Next came a second file of horsemen each in a quilted cotton cuirass, each with leather shield and iron lance.

The horses neighed and whinnied; they were all sweating.

The third group consisted of men with crossbows.

29

Following the commander came those of the enemy cities — Tepoztlan, Tlaxcalla, Tliliuhquitepec, Huexotzinco — each man arrayed for war in his quilted cotton armor, with his shield, with his bow. Each one's quiver bulged with arrows, some barbed, some obsidian-pointed, some blunted. Bent-kneed the men pranced whooping, shrieking as they struck hand against mouth, singing the Tocuillan song, bobbing their heads.

And with them mingled the carriers with baggage and rations on their backs in carrying frames, cages, baskets, bundles secured by tumplines. Some dragged the great lombard guns on their wooden wheels, singing as they forced them on.

Some just rested them on their shoulders.

They had quilted cotton armor reaching to the knees.

Fifth marched a group of arquebusiers.

At the very last came the commander, Cortés.

Following the commander came those of the enemy cities.

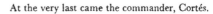

And with them mingled the carriers with baggage and rations on their backs.

Some dragged the great lombard guns on their wooden wheels.

31

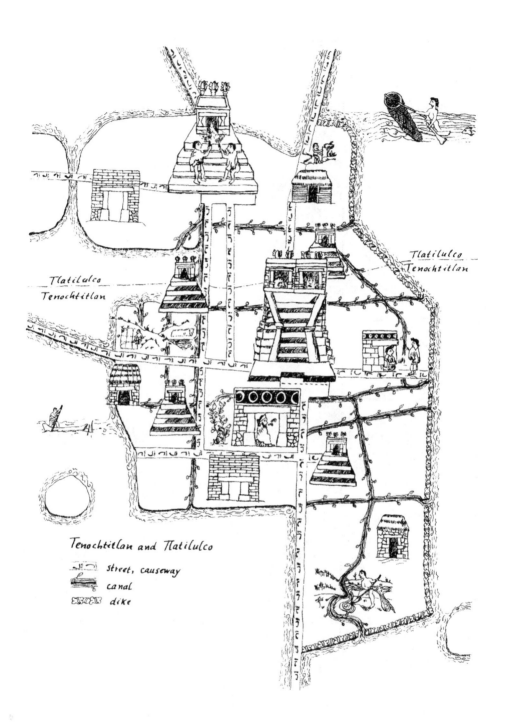

Tlatilulco
Tenochtitlan

Tlatilulco
Tenochtitlan

Tenochtitlan and Tlatilulco

street, causeway

canal

dike

IV

THE CAPTURE AND DEATH
OF MOCTEZUMA

Now Moctezuma peacefully, docilely, himself went to meet the Spaniards at Xoloco, at Uitzillan, the strategic point on the causeway from the mainland. He and a number of great lords and princes had arrayed themselves formally for the event. They went carrying gourd vases of helianthus and talauma surrounding popcorn flowers, yellow tobacco flowers, and cacao blossoms, as well as wreaths and garlands. Also they carried necklaces of gold, necklaces with pendants, and plaited neck bands.

There at Xoloco Moctezuma gave gifts to Cortés, the commander of the host. He gave him flowers; he decked him with necklaces. He had more golden necklaces laid out before him, all kinds of them, as gifts of greeting. He hung necklaces on some of Cortés's officers.

Then Cortés addressed Moctezuma: "Is this indeed you? Are you not Moctezuma?"

"Yes," Moctezuma answered; "I am he."

On this, he rose, to stand facing Cortés. He bowed deeply, drew him close, and stood firmly. Then he said,

"O our lord, you have tired yourself; you are weary. At last you have come to earth; you have come to govern your city of Mexico, to take your position of authority, which for a short time I have been keeping and guarding for you. Your former deputy governors have departed - - the rulers Itzcoatl, Moctezuma the Elder, Axayacatl, Tizoc,

Auitzotl, who also had come to keep watch, to govern the city of Mexico for you a short time ago and keep your people under their protection. Do the former rulers know what is happening in their absence? O that any of them might see, might wonder at what has befallen me — at what I am seeing now that they have gone. For I cannot be dreaming.

"For some time now have I been afflicted; I have gazed at the clouds, the mists, out of which you have come. And now this has come to pass. The departed rulers said as they left us that you would revisit your city, would return to your position of authority, and now it has so happened. You have come; you have tired yourself; you are weary. Rest yourself. Go into your palace; rest. Peace be with our lords."

When Moctezuma had finished his greeting, Marina then translated it for Cortés.
And when he heard what Moctezuma had
said, he spoke to Marina in his barbarous
tongue and said,

"Let Moctezuma be at ease; he need not
be frightened. We love him. We are indeed
satisfied now, having met him and heard
him. A long time have we wished to see
him; a long time have we hoped to look upon
his face. Now we have seen him; we have
come to his home in Mexico. When he
wishes, he can hear our words."

Then they took Moctezuma by the hand
and led him away. They stroked him with
their hands to express their love to him. And
they boldly looked at him; they examined
him. They kept moving about to do so,
continually mounting and dismounting their
horses to get a better view of him.

And various of the rulers of neighboring
cities accompanied him — Cacamatzin of
Texcoco, Tetlepanquetzatzin of Tlacopan,
the high warrior Itzquauhtzin, of Tlatelolco,
as well as Tepantemoctzin, who guarded
Moctezuma's treasure house in Tlatelolco.
Other noblemen were the high warriors
Atlixcatzin, Tepeuatzin, and Quetzalaztatzin. When Moctezuma was kept a captive
by the Spaniards, these noblemen went into
hiding not only to get away from the Spaniards but to express their disgust and anger
with Moctezuma.

They took Moctezuma by the hand and led him
away.

The Spaniards at once firmly siezed Moctezuma.

34

For as soon as they all came to and entered the palace, the Spaniards at once firmly seized Moctezuma. They continually kept him under close watch, never letting him out of their sight. Itzquauhtzin remained with him, but the others left; the Spaniards did not hold them.

When this had taken place, all the guns were fired. In great confusion everyone ran to one side or the other, scattered out of sight, jumped in all directions. It was as if we had had the breath knocked out of us, as if we had been stupefied, as if we had eaten the sacred mushrooms, as if we had seen a miracle. Fear was everywhere; it was as if all of us had lost our hearts. Long before nightfall there was apprehension, astonishment, terror. The people had been stunned.

Next day a proclamation called for all the things which the Spaniards needed: fine white tortillas, roast turkey, eggs, fresh water, firewood, charcoal, bowls, vessels, water jars and pitchers, cookery ware — all manner of crockery. This Moctezuma had commanded.

But when he called the noblemen to him, they would not come; they were angry. They never would come to him after that. He was not neglected; he was given all that he asked in food and drink and in water and fodder for the deer — that is, the horses. But he was no longer obeyed.

As soon as the Spaniards had quite settled themselves, they questioned Moctezuma about all the city's shields, emblems, and treasure; they continually importuned him; with no rest they sought gold. So Moctezuma then guided them as they surrounded and scattered about him. He was with them, showing them; they kept hold of him.

When they reached the treasure house, a building called Teocalco, the god's house, he then had all the brilliant things brought forth — the quetzal feather fanlike head ornaments; the emblems and shields; the gods' necklaces; the golden nose crescents, discs, and leg, arm, and forehead bands.

They at once removed the gold on the shields and emblems, and as they stripped it off, burned all the various precious things which remained. They set fire to it all. The gold the Spaniards melted into bars. Of jadeite ornaments they took whatever they thought was good. But the Tlaxcallans just stole the rest of the jadeite articles.[1]

---

[1] The Aztecs considered those articles made of quetzal feathers and jadeite as the most precious.

35

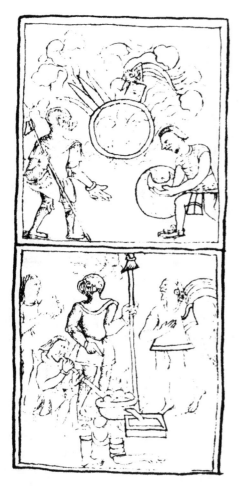

They at once removed the gold on the shields and emblems.

The gold the Spaniards melted into bars.

And the Spaniards kept walking everywhere, poking into and taking to pieces the hiding places and storehouses. They took all that they thought to be good.

Then they went to Moctezuma's private treasure house, a building called Totocalco, the bird house, in his own princely palace. They were tireless; in great contentment they clapped one another on the back; they all brightened up. When they reached the palace they dispersed into the treasure house, entering everywhere greedily, lustfully. Moctezuma's own property was then brought out — those things which were his exclusively — precious things like necklaces with pendants, arm bands tufted with quetzal feathers, golden arm bands, bracelets, golden anklets with shells, rulers' turquoise diadems, turquoise nose rods; no end of treasure. They took all, seized everything for themselves, appropriated all to themselves as if it were theirs.

When they had removed all the gold, they tossed all else away — those precious feathers, too — in the middle of the courtyard.

Then, the gold having been torn off Moctezuma's stock of finery, Marina had all the noblemen summoned. Standing upon a roof terrace, she addressed them:

"Mexicans, come here! The Spaniards have tired themselves. Bring them food, fresh water, and all that is needed. For they have wearied themselves, they are exhausted. . . .

"Why do you not wish to come? Can you be angry?"

But none of us Mexicans dared enter the palace. We were in terror, beside ourselves with fear. We were stunned. Fear stalked everywhere. It was as if a fierce beast were

36

enclosed there; it was as if the dangers of the night were there.

Yet we did not stop or interrupt leaving what the Spaniards required. We just left it in fear. We went up to the palace afraid, we ran off afraid as we left it. We would scatter it over the ground, and then run – – dash — back panting and trembling.

Marina had all the noblemen summoned. Standing upon a roof terrace she addressed them.

We did not stop or interrupt leaving what the Spaniards required. We just left it in fear.

Moctezuma's own property was brought out.

37

It then came to pass that Cortés had to leave for the coast to deal with Pánfilo de Narváez.[2] While he was away, Pedro de Alvarado asked Moctezuma what the Feast of Uitzilopochtli was like. He wanted, he said, to see how it was celebrated. So Moctezuma gave a command to those of his governors who could still enter the palace; they brought forth and passed on the word. When the instruction had come forth from where Moctezuma was imprisoned, preparations began.

The women who had fasted for a year[3] ground the amaranth seed, the fish amaranth seed, in the courtyard of the temple. To see them at work the Spaniards came forth elaborately dressed in battle array, in war array. They came up to and among the women, circling about them, looking at each one — looking into their faces. And when they had spent some time looking, they reentered the great palace.

As is known, the Spaniards would then have killed us if many of us warriors had been assembled there.

Pedro de Alvarado asked what the Feast of Uitzilopochtli was like.

---

[2] Since Cortés had disowned the control of Diego Vásquez de León, governor of Cuba, with whose authority the expedition had started and reached the mainland, Pánfilo de Narváez was sent in April, 1520, to reassert Velásquez's preeminence. Narváez was easily defeated and his followers won over. Cortés had meanwhile left his lieutenant Pedro de Alvarado in charge of the Spanish garrison in Tenochtitlan.

[3] Those who fasted for a year were especially dedicated to the service of the god Uitzilopochtli.

Moctezuma gave a command to his governors.

The Spaniards came up to the women, looking into their faces.

When finally the Feast of Toxcatl[4] came, toward sundown the women began to form the image of Uitzilopochtli in amaranth seed dough. They gave it the shape of a man; they shaped it on a framework of sticks — thorny ones, sticks forming angles. Then they pasted its head with feather down, gave the face its diagonal painting of stripes, and attached the serpent ear plugs of glued turquoise mosaic. From the serpent ear plugs hung golden rings of thorns cut in the shape of toes. His arrow-shaped nose rod of beaten gold set with stones was actually of thin plate painted as if with stones. From it hung what they called the thorn ring, painted with diagonal stripes, blue alternating with yellow. On his head arose his hummingbird disguise. Then followed a headdress of featherwork, cylindrical, rather pointed, rather narrow-based. Then, on the back of his head they set a ball of yellow parrot feathers from which hung a lock of child's hair. He had his black cape of nettles ornamented in five places with feathers, with eagle down. It was wrapped around him. Below, he was wrapped in a cape ornamented with severed heads and bones; above, he wore his sleeveless jerkin, a jerkin painted with severed heads, ears, hearts, entrails, livers, breasts, hands, and feet. He had his breech cloth, of the same design as the sleeveless jerkin. But his large breech cloth was only a paper one - - white paper a

---

[4] See *Introduction* and *Chronological Chart 2*. During the month of Toxcatl, one ritual honored the war god Tezcatlipoca, and a second ritual, here described, honored the god Uitzilopochtli and included the formation of his image. This ritual is described at length in Book II of Sahagún's *General History*.

39

fathom wide and twenty fathoms long, with
a blue stripe design. On his shoulders he
carried a blood banner as the burden upon
his back, a paper banner painted with stripes
of blood, on a staff with, at its point, a flint-
knife-shaped piece of paper painted with
stripes of blood. His shield was of stout reeds
decorated in four places with eagle down,
with feather tufts. They called the shield
teueuelli.[5] The shield banner was painted
like the blood banner. With his shield he
held four arrows. Over his left arm hung a
band made of strips of coyote fur, from
which hung strips of paper.

Early in the morning of the feast day,
those who had made vows to Uitzilopochtli
uncovered the figure's face. They stood in a
row before it; they offered it incense; before
it and on all sides they laid gifts — fasting
foods, rolls of amaranth seed dough. Later
they would take the figure up to Itepeyoc,
his temple. But now all the men, all of us
young seasoned warriors, were busy and
quite content in the progress of the feast, in
the observation of the feast, in order to show
it to the Spaniards — to give them something to wonder at.

Everyone was hastening to the courtyard
of temples for the dancing of the winding

---

[5] Teueuelli is the name of the shield carried by
the god Uitzilopochtli. It is recognizable by the four
or five down-feather tufts on its surface.

Toward sundown the women began to form the
image of Uitzilopochtli; they gave it the shape of
a man; they pasted its head with feather down.

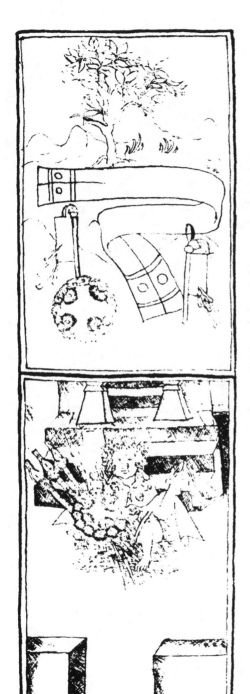

Those who had made vows uncovered the figure's face; they offered it incense; before it and on all sides they laid gifts.

His breech cloth was a paper one; his shield was of stout reeds decorated with eagle down, with feather tufts.

With his shield he held four arrows.

41

dance. As soon as enough assembled, we began; the singing had already started; now we were dancing. Those who had fasted twenty days and those who had fasted a whole year faced the rest of us. Those who acted as police had their pine cudgels, to stop any who tried to leave, though anyone who had to go off to urinate could indicate that he had to by taking off his cape of netting and his forked heron feather ornament. But if one were incorrigibly disobedient, if one

As soon as enough assembled, we began; the singing had already started.

Those who acted as police had their pine cudgels, to stop any who tried to leave.

Any who had to go off could indicate that by taking off his forked heron feather ornament.

were forward, impudent, they beat him soundly on the back, thighs, and shoulders. They put him, threw him, out by main force; he fell down, he went out on his ear. No one answered the police back.

The participants called Uitzilopochtli's elder brothers, those who had fasted a whole year, were regarded with real fear; they were regarded with terror, with dread. They were consequently treated with respect. Also those at the head, important personages, people who did great things: no one stopped them. All these could pass the police. But not the very raw youths. They were the ones who still had the lock of hair at the back of the head and the jar-shaped hair-do which meant that they had taken a war captive only with the aid of other warriors. Even those they called leaders, the unmarried leaders of the young men, who had in war succeeded in taking a captive or perhaps two, even these the police told, "Go on, you rogue! You are showing off to the people, not to us!"

So the feast began to be celebrated; already there was dancing, already there was song with dancing. The singing rolled like the breaking of the surf.

Having bided their time, having awaited the opportune moment, the Spaniards came forth to slay us. They wore battle array. They crowded wherever there was entry or exit to the courtyard of temples, the gateways called Quauhquiauac, Tecpantzinco, Acatl yiacapan, and Tezcacoac.[6] They

[6] The courtyard of temples was surrounded by a serpent wall, *coatepantli*. The four gateways are provisionally identified as Quauhquiauac to the south, Tecpantzinco to the west, Acatl yiacapan to the north, and Tezcacoac to the east.

blocked them; they stood in them. No one could get out. Then, each with shield, each with iron sword, they filed on foot into the courtyard to kill us.

They surrounded us dancers and then set upon the drummers. They first struck a drummer; they severed both his hands and cut off his head, which fell to the ground some distance away. Then they charged the crowd with their iron lances and hacked us with their iron swords. They slashed the

They first struck a drummer; they severed both his hands.

They hacked us with their iron swords.

43

backs of some, so that their entrails poured out. They cut to pieces the heads of others — pulverized them. They hacked at the shoulders of others, splitting their bodies open; or at their shanks, or at their thighs, or at their abdomens, breaking out their entrails, which dragged as they tried to run. But if any tried to run, the Spaniards stabbed and struck them down.

A few were able to escape up over the wall. Some fled into the adjacent administrative area buildings. Some of us, playing dead, crawled in among the bodies of the slain and escaped — unless the Spaniards saw one breathe and stabbed him.

The blood of the young warriors ran like water; it gathered in pools. A foul stench arose from and spread about the carnage. Blood and entrails lay everywhere. And the Spaniards began to hunt them out of the administrative area buildings, dragging out and killing anyone they could find. They got in everywhere, even starting to take those buildings to pieces as they searched.

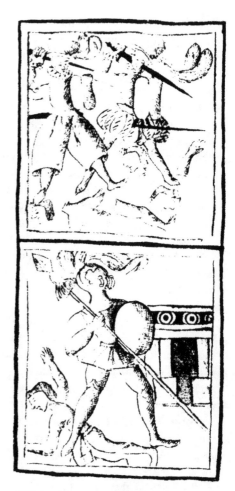

They slashed the backs of some; they cut to pieces the heads of others.

If any tried to run, the Spaniards stabbed and struck them down.

The blood of the young warriors ran like water; it gathered in pools.

44

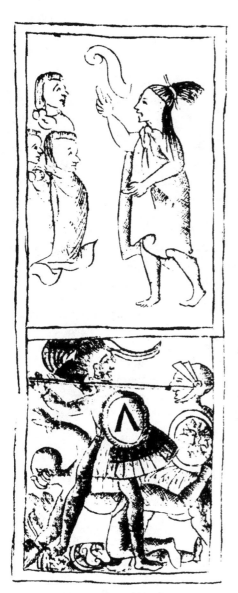

As soon as it was realized that the massacre was taking place, a shouting arose.

We shot at the Spaniards with barbed arrows, with darts, with tridents.

As soon as it was realized that the massacre was taking place, a shouting arose: "Warriors! Mexicans! Come quickly — in war array! Bring your emblems, shields, arrows! Come! Hurry! Already the warriors have died, perished, been annihilated! Mexicans! Warriors!"

And the outcry continued, the shouting, the shrieks throbbing as hands kept striking lips.

Quickly were forces marshalled. Determined, the brave warriors came with shields and arrows, and fought. We shot at the Spaniards with barbed arrows, with darts, with tridents, with arrows of barbed point and of broad, obsidian point, a mass of yellow reeds which cast a shadow over the Spaniards.

Thus open war broke out. The Spaniards had to take to the shelter of the stone walls of the great palace, from behind which they shot back iron arrows and fired their guns.

Also they put Moctezuma in irons.

Meanwhile, the bodies of the brave warriors who had died were brought forth from the courtyard of the temples and identified, their mothers and fathers standing by and wailing. After they had been wept over, they were taken first to their homes and then back to the courtyard of the temples. There they brought the bodies together. Some they then

burned in a place called Quauhxicalco, the eagle vessel; some they burned only at the various houses in which the young men were educated to be warriors.[7]

In the late afternoon light, just before sunset, Itzquauhtzin shouted forth from a company of Spaniards and Mexicans on the palace roof terrace:

"Mexicans! Men of Tenochtitlan! Men of Tlatelolco! Your ruler, the lord of men, Moctezuma, implores you. He says, 'Listen, Mexicans! We are not equal to the Spaniards! Abandon the battle! Still your arrows, hold back your shields! Otherwise, evil will be the fate of the miserable old men and women, of the people, of babes in arms, of the toddlers, of the infants crawling on the ground or still in the cradle!'

"He tells you that we are not the Spaniards' equals, that we should stop fighting, because they have put him in irons — have put his feet in irons!'"

But upon this the Mexicans raised a clamor. They berated him. They were furious with rage. One was so much inflamed that he shouted,

---

[7] Four places were named Quauhxicalco in the temple square and are mentioned in Book II of Sahagún's *General History*. The youth houses, military centers, were nearby.

The Spaniards had to take to the shelter of the stone walls of the great palace.

They put Moctezuma in irons.

The bodies of the brave warriors who had died were brought forth.

"What does Moctezuma say, you villain? Aren't you one of his warriors?"

In the increasing outcry which followed, arrows fell upon the roof terrace. The Spaniards protected Moctezuma and Itzquauhtzin with their shields so that the Mexicans might not injure them. But the Mexicans were beside themselves with rage because the Spaniards had completely annihilated our brave warriors --- had slain them without warning by treachery.

The lull that followed was not because of the Mexicans' weakness. They still watched the various points where one might secretly enter the palace -- where one might secretly smuggle in tortillas. The Mexicans completely cut them off from supplies from outside; no one could leave them anything. They would starve them.

If anyone were seen, were espied, trying to inform those in the palace, to warn them, to take in any food secretly, right then and there they killed him. They hit him on the head, or they stoned him.

Once some Mexicans carrying in rabbit skins let fall information that through them some had secretly gotten in. Those who had taken the skins in were underlings, emissaries of the stewards of Ayotzintepec and Chinantla. They breathed their last right then and there; that was the last thing they did. At the canal's edge each one was hit on the head

"Mexicans! Your ruler, the lord of men, Moctezuma, implores you."

If anyone were seen trying to take in any food, they killed him.

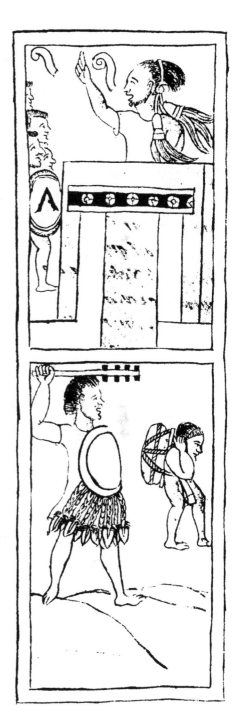

with wooden clubs. And strict orders were issued to watch every canal, to guard every road thoroughly and well.

In fact, as it turned out, the people of Tenochtitlan were really hurting themselves. Quite mistakenly had they seized these underlings. They had jumped to a conclusion - - "This is the one!" - - and at once killed him.

Coming upon anyone wearing a fine lip rod was enough reason to seize and kill him. They would say, "Here is one who has entered the palace to give food to Moctezuma." Or they would stop anyone dressed in a servant's century plant fiber cape. Him they would also quickly seize. "This wretch goes bearing words of scandal," they would say. "He takes them to Moctezuma; he sees Moctezuma!"

In vain would one try to escape. He would say, "What do you want, Mexicans? I am not doing anything." They would reply, "You are, too, villain! Aren't you a servant?" And then and there they would kill him.

They spied on everyone; they were suspicious of people. That was all they did. Those Mexicans just watched everyone. They punished many for purely imaginary crimes; they killed them treacherously for things they did not do.

Consequently, servants hid themselves away and took refuge. They were no more to be seen. They lived beside themselves with fear, lest they fall into the people's hands.

On besieging the Spaniards, we fought them only seven days of the twenty-three that they were shut in. During that time we dredged each canal, made it wider, made it deeper, made its sides steeper. Everywhere we made the canals as difficult and dangerous as possible. On the roads we built ramparts, barricades. We made the passages between houses as difficult as possible.

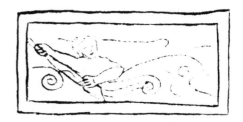

By then, Cortés, returning from his action against Pánfilo de Narváez, was just setting out from Tepeyacac. He had with him many more Spaniards and a host of Tlaxcallans and Cempoallans - - an abundance, a super-abundance. Not only were they entering Mexican territory, but these Cempoallans and Tlaxcallans were coming as warriors, carrying emblems, arrayed for war, with shield and obsidian-bladed sword in hand, with hand staff shouldered. They raised a great column of dust, and their faces were caked with dust and ashes. They were covered and cloaked with dust. And they were moving fast, at a run. Hastening, they went each one shouting, "Hurry up, Tlaxcallans! Hurry up, Cempoallans!"

The Mexicans had decided among themselves to remain out of sight, silent. So they hid, took refuge, leaving the city apparently dead. But they remained watching through the door openings, through the gaps and holes in the walls of houses lining the roadside. Many waited farther back, where they could not see.

If the Spaniards had known how many of our brave warriors there were in some places, they could have had little doubt that the Mexicans would soon resume the outbreak of war.

Things being as they were, Cortés entered the palace. The Spaniards fired their guns.

Then the Mexicans came out with war cries and joined battle. There was fighting. Arrows and stones rained on the Spaniards. These returned volleys of iron bolts and shots.

Many of us Mexicans were felled. The crossbowmen aimed well; the bolts accounted for whomever they pierced. As they flew through the air, they went humming; they sped with a great rush, and not in vain. All struck their men—pierced them through. And the guns were well trained and aimed at the insurgents. On hearing the shot discharged, we would all fall and cower on the ground. The shots came upon one unaware; before one knew it, one was killed. As many as the missiles overtook, so many died when they struck the forehead, the back of the head, the heart, the chest, the abdomen — any vital part. If they struck the thighs or the shoulder, the men might not die; they could recover.

When we Mexicans realized how the iron bolts and shots struck, we would jump aside. We learned to be watchful, careful.

Cortés was just setting out from Tepeyacac.

He had with him a host of Tlaxcallans and Cempoallans.

49

After four days of this, some select, chosen warriors, possessors of emblems, in whose faces was war, climbed up to the top of the pyramid temple, enticing the Spaniards to follow. They took up two beams and a number of cylindrical oak logs, called gods' wood, planning to roll them down upon the enemy. The Spaniards climbed up slowly, in order, in file, the arquebusiers taking the lead. They did not stop as they fired their arquebuses at the warriors. Next came crossbowmen; then swordsmen; and finally the lancers, the halberdiers.

But it did no good to throw the beams and thick oak logs upon the Spaniards. They just warded them off with their shields and kept on climbing after the warriors to the top, there striking, stabbing, piercing them repeatedly. So the warriors threw themselves down to the landings of the pyramid temple, scattering like black ants. The rest the Spaniards hurled down from the temple top — every one. Not one escaped. Then the Spaniards quickly reentered the palace and shut themselves in.

All this took place at noon.

Then the dead were identified and taken out, and the bodies were burned at the various houses where warriors were schooled.

It was after another four days that the Spaniards threw the dead bodies of Mocte-

So they hid, took refuge.

The Spaniards fired their guns.

The warriors threw themselves down to the landings of the pyramid temple.

zuma and Itzquauhtzin out of the palace, at a place called Teoayoc, the stone turtle carving. As soon as they were recognized, men quickly took up Moctezuma's body and carried it to Copulco, placed it on a pile of wood, and fired it. The flames crackled and flared up into many tongues; the body seemed to lie sizzling, sending up a foul stench.

As he burned, onlookers berated him; their good will had given way to fury. "This blockhead," they said, "terrorized the world. He kept the world in dread, in fear. If anyone offended this man even a little, he at once did away with him. Many did he punish for imagined misdoings, for deeds that were mere fabrications of words." And they would groan, cry out, and shake disapproving heads.

Itzquauhtzin's body they carried off in a boat to Tlatelolco, of which he had been ruler. For him they felt great pity, great compassion. No one berated him; no one scorned him. Tears flowed.

"This personage, the high warrior Itzquauhtzin," they said, "tired himself out. He was unfortunate, with Moctezuma. How he must have tired himself out on our account during the time Moctezuma was alive!"

Then they arrayed him in the palace flag and the accustomed paper wrappings, made offerings to him, and took him to the courtyard of temples, to a place called Quauhxicalco, the eagle vessel, to burn him with great honors.[9]

There followed four further days of fighting. Then after remaining shut in the great palace seven days the Spaniards broke out again, to look around, going as far as Mazatzintamalco. They gathered the green stalks of corn, which was just maturing — gathering it for fodder, just like enemies. It was a hasty sally; they no more than arrived there than they quickly returned and entered the building. The sun was high when they set forth; it was setting on their return.

[8] Native sources almost all say that Moctezuma, Itzquauhtzin, and others were stabbed or strangled by the Spaniards. Spanish sources attribute the death of Moctezuma to his being stoned while on the rooftop trying to pacify the Aztecs.

[9] The high respect shown for Itzquauhtzin by those of Tlatelolco probably reflects local reaction to the subjugated status of the place with respect to Mexico. As for Moctezuma, some sources stress his arrogance and capricious meting of punishments, and of course he could not evade ultimate responsibility for admitting the Spaniards into Mexico, whatever the facts really were.

Itzquauhtzin's body they carried off in a boat to Tlatelolco.

They took him to the courtyard of temples to burn him with great honors.

The Spaniards threw the bodies of Moctezuma and Itzquauhtzin out of the palace.

Men quickly took up Moctezuma's body.

They carried it to Copulco, placed it on a pile of wood, and fired it.

V

THE ESCAPE OF THE SPANIARDS

THAT night, at midnight, the enemy came
out, crowded together, the Spaniards in the
lead, the Tlaxcallans following, covering the
rear - - like their walls, their ramparts. They
carried a wooden platform with them,
placed it over the canal, and crossed over
upon it. Screened by a fine drizzle, a fine
sprinkle of rain, they were able undetected
to cross the canals of Tecpantzinco, Tzapo-
tlan, and Atenchicalco. But as they reached
the fourth canal, that of Mixcoatechialtitlan,
just as they were crossing, a woman drawing
water saw them.

"Mexicans! Come, all of you," she
shouted. "They are already leaving! They
are already secretly getting out!"

Then a watcher at the top of the temple
of Uitzilopochtli also shouted, and his cries
pervaded the entire city. Everyone heard
him.

"Brave warriors! Mexicans!" he called.
"Your enemy already leaves! Hurry with
the shield-boats and along the road!"

Then there was a general outcry. The
shield-boatmen broke forth, poling furiously.
Boats kept striking against each other as they
reached Mictlantonco macuilcuitlapilco.
There from two sides the shield-boatmen
pressed against the Spaniards as the shield-
boats of Tenochtitlan joined forces with
those of Tlatelolco. Other warriors hurried

The enemy came out, crowded together, the Spaniards in the lead.

"Mexicans! Come, all of you," she shouted.

53

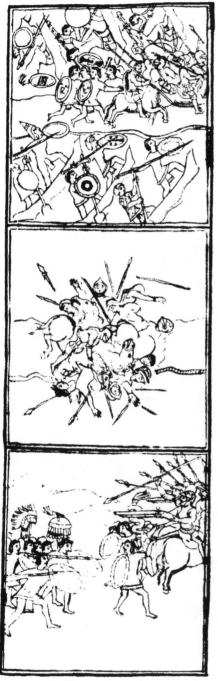

on foot, going direct to Nonoalco or Tlaco-pan, to ambush the rout if it reached that far.

From both sides the shield-boatmen hurled their barbed spears on the Spaniards. The Spaniards shot arrows and iron bolts at the Mexicans and fired their guns at them. Men died on both sides; Spaniards and Tlaxcallans were pierced by arrows; Mexi-cans were pierced by arrows. Then, when the Spaniards reached the Tolteca canal, they seemed to fall into a chasm. They filled it. It seemed as if everyone fell into it — Tlaxcallans, T'liliuhquitepecans, Spaniards, their horses, their women. The canal was filled, crammed with them. Those who came along behind walked over on men, on corpses.

At Petlacalco, where there was another canal, there quite unobtrusively, quietly, slowly, cautiously, they again crossed on the wooden platform. There they recovered a little—restored themselves—regained their manhood.

By the time they reached Popotlan, it was dawn. That gave them some courage. But also they could be seen from afar, and we Mexicans took after them with a roar, sur-rounding them, taking Tlaxcallan and Span-

From two sides the shield-boatmen pressed against the Spaniards.

When the Spaniards reached the Tolteca canal, they seemed to fall in a chasm.

We drove the Spaniards to Tlacopan, pursuing them hotly.

ish captives, killing others. Mexicans and Tlatelolcans too were killed. There were deaths on both parts. But we drove the Spaniards to Tlacopan, pursuing them hotly, and continued to drive them to Tliliuhcan, to Xocotl ihiouican, to Xoxocotla.

There Moctezuma's son Chimalpopoca died; he was found lying pierced by a barbed spear, wounded by many blows. There also died Tlaltecatzin, a Tepaneca lord guiding the Spaniards, pointing the right roads, easing the way for them.

After Xoxocotla they forded a small river, the Tepzolatl, climbed up to Acueco, and finally rested at Otoncalpulco, where, in the courtyard, there were wooden palisades. There they could restore and mend themselves. There the people of Teocalhueyacan came to them and guided them forth.

Their leader, whom they commonly called lord of men, was named Otoncoatl. They arrived carrying food — fine white tortillas; turkeys, uncooked, stewed, and roasted, as well as some live ones; eggs; tuna cactus fruit. These they set forth before Cortés.

"You have tired yourselves," they said. "Our lords the gods are wearied. They should rest; they should restore themselves. Peace be with them."

They were answered by Marina, who said, "My governors, Cortés asks whence you have come, where your home is."

"May our lord listen," they answered. "We come from his house in Teocalhueyacan. We are Teocalhueyacanians."

"Very well," she said. "We are obliged to you. We shall go there tomorrow; we shall sleep there."

Meanwhile in Mexico, when dawn had broken, men began to remove the bodies of all the Tlaxcallans, Cempoallans, and Spaniards who had fallen into the Tolteca canal chasm, as well as into the Petlacalco and Mictlantonco canals. They took them away in boats and laid each one out impaled upon the reeds and rushes of the banks. And they took out the bodies of the women—despoiled of their goods, naked, yellowish-skinned. The Spaniards they stretched out apart, arranged in separate rows, their bodies white like reed shoots, like white century plant roots, like white corn stalks. And they brought up the deer-which-carried-men-upon-their-backs, called horses.

And all the goods which they had been carrying on their backs or had been dressed in, all were taken. They were appropriated by whoever found them, as if they were his because of merit. Whoever found something took it up, put it upon his back, and carried it home. The booty included all that had been dropped, abandoned in the terror of the rout. Much of it was war goods:

55

lombard guns, arquebuses, gunpowder, iron
swords, halberds, iron bolts, iron arrows
were strewn about. Also taken by the finders
as if theirs because merited were the iron
helmets, corselets, chain mail, and shields,
along with the gold in bars, discs, and dust,
and the necklaces with pendants.

When all the larger things had been taken
up, many still dispersed in the water scratching the bottom for more with their hands or
their feet.

It was plain that whoever had survived
to get away had been at the head of the
column. Those who followed were the ones
who fell into the chasm; all of them had
died. It was as if a mountain of men had
been laid down; they had pressed against
one another, smothered one another.

At Acueco the Spaniards slept until,
toward dawn, they arose, arrayed themselves for war, and disposed themselves in
battle order. As they did so, the Mexicans
shouted and yelled at them, not coming up
to them but keeping their distance.

Men began to remove the bodies; they laid each
one out.

All the goods were taken. Whoever found something took it up and carried it home.

Many dispersed in the water scratching the bottom
for more.

56

The Spaniards continued to an isolated place called Calacoayan, on the top of a low, rounded hill where there were ridges of rocks. There they at once killed the inhabitants — speared them. They did not warn them; they killed them without notice, vented their wrath upon them, took their pleasure with them. Then, coming down to the small, flat plain called Tizapan, they climbed up to Teocalhueyacan,[1] where they settled in the administrative area buildings of this Otomí village.

They arrived at about noon. Everything was at hand, everything was arranged for them: the food, the turkeys, etc. They gave the Spaniards great contentment and went among them quite peacefully. They gave them all they asked for: fodder for the deer they rode, that is, the horses; water; degrained corn; ears of corn, raw, cooked, roasted; green corn tortillas and tamales; squashes cut in sections. They kept pressing these upon them, wishing to become their friends.

Now the Teocalhueyacanians were related to the Tliliuhquitepecans who were with Cortés; the native land, the foundation place, the seat of the Tliliuhquitepecans was Teocalhueyacan. Here the two related branches consulted among themselves, came to an arrangement, and determined to meet with the god, that is, with Cortés, and beseech him and the other gods, the Spaniards, in these words:

"The gods have come to their poor home in Teocalhueyacan. Here we, their vassals, greet and beseech them to hear us Teocal-

They at once killed the inhabitants — speared them.
They climbed up to Teocalheuyacan.

---

[1] Teocalhueyacan was an Otomí village adjacent to Tlalnepantla.

hueyacanians and Tliliuhquitepecans. Moctezuma and the Mexicans have given us much pain, much vexation. They have kept us in affliction up to our very noses. They imposed a tribute upon us. They have become our rulers. If the gods, the Spaniards, should abandon us in haste, if they should go and delay in returning, so perverse are the Mexicans that they will kill us. For indeed the Mexicans are surpassingly perverse." [2]

When Marina had interpreted for Cortés, he replied, "Tell the Teocalhueyacanians not to worry. I shall not delay; I shall soon return and find them here. This will be the place where judgment is made, and the Mexicans will be destroyed. Do not be alarmed."

The promise brought much contentment to the Teocalhueyacanians, not to mention pride and even arrogance. Because of it they stood up thinking well of themselves, considering themselves well favored. They were self-satisfied, proud, as if convinced that the promise was already fact.

When all had slept, it was well before dawn that the flutes were blown and the war

---

[2] This fear of the Teocalhueyacanians reflects the native pattern of conquest. They feared that the Spaniards would return to their homeland content to exact tribute from them, thus allowing the Mexicans to reconquer them.

They gave the Spaniards great contentment; they gave them all they asked for.

The two related branches determined to meet with Cortés and beseech him.

The flutes were blown and war drum beaten.

drum beaten. The Spaniards arose, arrayed themselves, and crowded into the road to leave. It was early when they left, and after following the road a short time they reached Tepotzotlan; but so great had the Spaniards' victories been that the Tepotzotlanians broke away, ran, and abandoned the town. Some of them made for the forest, some for the mountains, some for the gorges, saving only their bodies, for in their haste they left all their goods scattered about.

The Spaniards entered the palace and camped in the courtyard grouped and huddled together. For they too went in fear.

The following morning they again broke their fast early. As they departed, the Tepotzotlanians pursued them shouting and bellowing at them — from a distance, for if one dared go up as if to interrogate them, the Spaniards speared him; no one saved the speared one.

Next they reached and camped in Citlaltepec. Its people, too, fled; the common folk did not wait for them. The warriors and inhabitants took pains not to show themselves; they stayed behind rock cactuses, century plants, piles of earth, crags; for the Spaniards were too strong to resist.

So great had the Spaniards' victories been that the Tepotzotlanians broke away, ran, and abandoned the town.

As they departed, the Tepotzotlanians pursued them.

The warriors and inhabitants took pains not to show themselves.

There too they slept until the next dawn, in whose warm light they arose, ate, and started on to Xoloc. Like the other places, it also was abandoned to the Spaniards. No one awaited them; houses were vacant. The inhabitants had gone above to Mt. Xoloc, where they could lie hidden watching the Spaniards in the high plains, the gullies, the canyons that they passed through. For they dreaded the Spaniards; they were afraid lest they spring unaware on them.

As they broke their fast and began to move in the early dawn, on each side of the road advanced the deer — those called horses, on which men rode — while all who carried burdens upon their backs marched within the files, surrounded. As soon as they were through with the place in which they had camped, they set fire to the Otomí temples, to all the temples; they burned, crackled, as the blaze, the tongues, the sheets of flame rose spreading smoke. Then they marched off, with the people of Tepotzotlan yelling and shouting at them — from a distance.

From here the enemy went on until they stopped at the foot of Mt. Aztaquemecan, in a place called Zacamulco, above which was an Otomí temple upon a rounded hill. There they installed themselves in the houses which the inhabitants had again left vacant. No longer did people come to meet them; the houses everywhere lay silent, lay clear as they came up to them.

The inhabitants had gone above to Mt. Xoloc, where they could lie hidden.

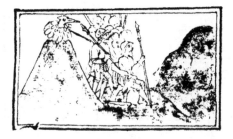

The enemy went on until they stopped at the foot of Mt. Aztaquemecan.

60

Just at this time our Mexican forces caught up with the Spaniards, to try to intercept them as they camped at the foot of Mt. Tonan. At dawn, the Spaniards attired themselves and ate; we Mexicans likewise attired ourselves, ate, and drank the war ration of pinole mixed with water. Then some climbed up the mountain to spy on the Spaniards and be ready for them as they made ready to go.

When the Spaniards were on the road, the spies shouted, "Mexicans! The enemy is already going! Let us get into our war gear and move in on them together! Let no one stay behind!" Then there was running hither and thither in pursuit.

Seeing them, the Spaniards stopped and checked themselves, to size up the situation. As they hesitated, we Mexicans fell upon them so suddenly as to enclose them completely. But then followed repeated spearing and striking down of Mexicans and Tlatelolcans, who had thus cast themselves into the hands of the Spaniards -— who, except for a few, had only followed death. Those who remained at a distance were still safe.

When the Spaniards had wiped out this Mexican force, had taken their pleasure with it, they went on, those carrying burdens upon their backs marching last. From this time on, we do not know where they slept. This was the point at which we Mexicans turned back, turned away from the Spaniards' footsteps.

Instead, we thereupon stopped to identify each of the brave warriors who had died, speared, in the battle. Right there we burned them all; then we gathered up their charred bones, heaped them up, and buried them.

When the Spaniards were on the road, the spies shouted, "Mexicans! The enemy is already going!"

Here follows a reckoning of the time since the Spaniards came into Mexico.

They entered on the day One Wind of the ceremonial calendar, and in the year One Reed on the day before the tenth of the month Quecholli of the civil calendar; when the ceremonial calendar day Two House had been completed, then it was the tenth of Quecholli. On the very day after Quecholli ended, then Panquetzaliztli followed as the next month with its twenty days. Then Ti-

titl: twenty; then Izcalli tlami: twenty; then
the Nemontemi days: five; then Atl caualo
or Quauitl eua: twenty, which took hold of
and began the new year; then Tlacaxipeualiztli: another twenty; then Tozoztontli:
another twenty; then Uei tozoztli: another
twenty; then Toxcatl: twenty more. In that
month perished our brave warriors cut to
pieces in the massacre of the Mexicans. Next
came Etzalqualiztli: twenty; then Tecuilhuitontli. Just at that time the Spaniards
broke out and disappeared from our knowledge during the night. We did not think
they would leave after dark. If all the days
completed are added up, they come to two
hundred and thirty-five.

They had been our friends one hundred
and ninety-five days. They had been our
enemies forty days.

And when the Spaniards thus disappeared, we thought they had gone for good,
nevermore to return.

"Let us get into our war gear and move in on them
together!"

Then followed repeated spearing and striking
down of Mexicans and Tlatelolcans.

We stopped to identify each of the brave warriors
who had died; we burned them all.

62

VI

THE RETURN OF THE SPANIARDS

Once again the temples could be swept out — the rubbish in each picked up, the dirt removed; they could be adorned, ornamented. The month of Uei tecuilhuitl came, and Mexicans once again observed its feast on the twentieth day. They attired all the images of the gods; they ornamented them with precious feathers, hung them with necklaces, put turquoise mosaic masks on them, and dressed them in godly ornaments — the quetzal feather one, the yellow parrot feather one, the eagle feather one, all precious goods which the great noblemen guarded.

After the month of Uei tecuilhuitl, Tlaxochimaco came with its twenty days. Xocotl uetzi followed also with its twenty. With Ochpaniztli we passed the fourth score of days; with Teotl eco the fifth score; Tepeilhuitl, the sixth score; Quecholli, the seventh score. This would have completed a year of the Spaniards in Mexico, except that they had already gone. Then came Panquetzaliztli, the eighth score; Atemoztli, the ninth; Tititl, the tenth; Izcalli tlami, the eleventh score. Nemontemi then came with its five days, and Atl caualo with its twelfth score of days; Tlacaxipeualiztli, thirteenth score; Tozoztontli, fourteenth; Uei tozoztli, Toxcatl, Etzalqualiztli; Tecuilhuitontli, the eighteenth score of days, making a year since the Spaniards had died in the Tolteca canal.

Once again the temples could be swept out.

They attired all the images of the gods.

63

But it was when the year was in its eleventh score, in Izcalli, that we once again saw the Spaniards. They were approaching from the direction of Quauhtitlan. They kept right on to make camp at Tlacopan, where they remained seven days. Then they went away for forty days. Once again they approached, coming quickly toward Quauhtitlan. Their only exploit was to kill people in Tlaliztacapan and Iztacalla; about four hundred Tlatelolcans died.

It was after two more sets of twenty days, in the month of Toxcatl,[1] in the second year after the brave warriors died in the courtyard of temples, that they held consultations, councils of war, about us.

But at about the time that the Spaniards had fled from Mexico, before they had once again risen against us, there came a great sickness, a pestilence, the smallpox. It started in the month of Tepeilhuitl and spread over the people with great destruction of men.[2]

It caused great misery. Some people it covered with pustules, everywhere, the face, the head, the breast, etc. Many indeed perished from it. They could not walk; they could only lie at home in their beds, unable to move, to raise themselves, to stretch out on their sides, or lie face down, or upon their backs. If they stirred they cried out with great pain. Like a covering over them were the pustules. Indeed many people died of them. But many just died of hunger. There were so many deaths that there was often no one to care for the sick; they could not be attended.

On some the pustules broke out far apart. They did not cause much suffering, nor did many die of them. Many others were harmed by them on their faces; face and nose were left roughened. Some had their eyes injured by them; they were blinded. Many were crippled by it — though not entirely.

The pestilence lasted through sixty day signs before it diminished. When it was realized that it was beginning to end, it was going toward Chalco. The pestilence became prevalent in the month of Teotl eco; it was diminishing in Panquetzaliztli. The brave Mexican warriors were indeed weakened by it.

It was after all this had happened that the Spaniards came back.

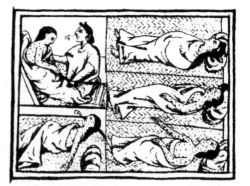

There came a great sickness, a pestilence, the smallpox.

---

[1] The native tally is confusing in the Aztec text of this passage. We think our reading in the translation may be correct.

[2] Upon the death of Moctezuma, Cuitlauac became the tenth ruler of the Mexicans. He reigned eighty days. The smallpox epidemic started in his reign.

They began moving in from Texcoco, setting forth by way of Quauhtitlan. They established themselves in Tlacopan. Here responsibilities were divided among the Spanish leaders. Pedro de Alvarado's forces blocked the Tlacopan road leading to Tlatelolco. Cortés, with headquarters in Coyoacan, undertook to dominate it as well as the road leading from Acachinanco to Tenochtitlan; for he knew that the Mexicans were great warriors.

It was in Nextlatilco, or Ilyacac, that war first burst out anew. The Spaniards quickly came to Nonoalco; the brave warriors following after them made them turn their backs. None of the Mexicans died. The brave warriors fought from boats; the shield-boatmen rained arrows on the Spaniards, and it was we Mexicans who entered Nonoalco. Cortés, advancing along the Acachinanco road, thereupon threw his Spaniards against the Mexicans. Many times did the battle flare as Mexican warriors kept contending against him.

They began moving in from Texcoco, setting forth by way of Quauhtitlan.

It was in Nextlatilco, or Ilyacac, that war first burst out anew.

Cortés, advancing along the Acachinanco road, thereupon threw his Spaniards against the Mexicans.

Now also the Spaniards made boats in Texcoco in order to attack Mexico. Twelve of them had come from there, for the time remaining assembled at Acachinanco, where Cortés then joined them. Soon with two boats he started testing out where he could enter Mexico: where the canals were straight and deep enough, and where too shallow, lest they be grounded. But here the canals were too winding, too sharply curved. But they got them in at last by forcing them through the road which led from Xoloco.

Then they held a council of war and determined upon putting all Mexicans to the spear. So they resolved. They readied

themselves. They carried guns. They bore a large cotton banner at their head. They advanced calmly, untroubled, beating the drums, blowing trumpets and flutes.

Quite silently did the two boats sail toward Zoquipan, holding themselves to one side of the canal, since a group of houses stood on the other. They moved apace, giving battle; men fell dead on both sides; attackers and attacked both took captives. Seeing this, the people of Tenochtitlan who lived in Zoquipan fled in terror — young, old, babes in arms. The common folk just all took to the water. A wailing arose. Those who had boats filled them with their babies and poled away — poled furiously. Nothing else did they take; in their haste they abandoned all their scattered goods, poor stuff which our foes nevertheless looted, taking whatever they found, capes large and small, emblems, two-toned drums, vertical drums. . . .

But if the people of Tenochtitlan evacuated Zoquipan, the Tlatelolcans, arriving in shield-boats, fought the Spaniards there.

The Spaniards made boats in Texcoco in order to attack Mexico.

They bore a large cotton banner at their head.

The Spaniards sailed up to Xoloco, where the wall stretched across the causeway; they fired their big gun.

Those who had boats filled them with their babies and poled away.

Next the Spaniards sailed up to Xoloco, where the wall stretched across the causeway road. They fired their big gun at it. The first shot did not break it down; the second did; the third and fourth tumbled it to the ground forever.

Then the two boats turned upon the Tlatelolcan shield-boatmen. Little contest in the water followed. Guns filled the prows of the Spanish vessels; they fired where the Mexican boats lay massed. The Mexican boats would lift their prows, veer sideways, and sink. And as for the iron crossbows, no one the Spaniards could aim at escaped; he then and there breathed his last. Many men thus died.

However, when we Mexicans had learned to judge how the shots from the guns and the bolts from the crossbows would fall, none of us ever ran a direct course. We would always zig-zag from one side to the other. Likewise, when we saw that the big gun shot was about to fall, we all would crouch or stretch out on the ground.

But the brave warriors quickly dispersed among the houses. The wide road was left clear.

After this the Spaniards reached Uitzillan, where another wall cut the road. Many Mexicans lay crouched, hidden by it. For a short time the Spanish brigantines were stuck, grounded there; while they freed themselves they prepared the guns. At the first shot, the wall fell to pieces; the shot broke through at the back. At the second, it collapsed to the ground. It was thrown down in various places, broken, torn open; the road was left clear. The brave warriors who had been protected by the wall at once scattered — fled in fear.

Now that the area was clear, the Spaniards' various allied people quickly proceeded to fill each canal. They leveled them with stones, with adobes, with logs. Thus they blocked the waterways. Then the horsemen, perhaps ten of them, passed over, following after the others.

Here some Tlatelolcans who had dashed into the palace once occupied by Moctezuma ran out in great fear. But they came encountering the horsemen, who speared one. The Tlatelolcan, however, was able still to grasp the iron lance until his friends ran up, tore it from the rider's hands, threw him on his back, and overcame him. On the ground they repeatedly struck him on the back of the head. He died.

But the Spaniards determined among themselves to advance together and moved on against Quauhquiauac, the eagle gate[3] of the courtyard of temples, taking with them their lombard gun and its paraphernalia. This they put down at the eagle gate. While they did this, the great brave warriors in vain hid themselves behind the stone columns — eight, arranged in two rows — and upon the roof of the Coacalli, the snake house. There on the roof terrace they lay crowded. But none of the brave warriors ventured beyond.

The Spaniards moved not at all. They only fired the gun. And when they did so, it became very dark. Smoke spread everywhere. Those hiding among the stone columns took flight; those crouched on the roof terrace threw themselves down from there. They all ran off.

Then the Spaniards took up the gun and carried it to the gladiatorial sacrifice stone and laid it there. At the summit of the pyramid temple of Uitzilopochtli the priests watched unable to do anything, beating, furiously beating the two-toned drum. Two Spaniards climbed up the pyramid, struck all the priests, and threw them down from the top.

On this, all the brave warriors jumped ashore from the boats in which they had been fighting while the young boys poled them; we warriors studied the spaces between the buildings and shouted, "Hasten, brave warriors! Hasten here!" Seeing that we were nearly upon them, the Spaniards crouched down, turned their backs, and ran. There were flights of arrows on both sides; there were volleys of stones on both sides. We warriors afterwards went on to Xoloco and stopped there to mend, to restore ourselves. Then we turned back. The Spaniards also withdrew; they went back to their quarters in Acachinanco. But in their haste they had left their gun on the gladiatorial sacrifice stone. We warriors seized it; we worried it along to Tetamazolco, where we dropped it into the lake.

---

[3] It was called the eagle gate because in that place stood a carved stone eagle, as tall as a man, flanked on one side by a jaguar and on the other by a wolf, both of stone. (This explanation appears as an "aside" in the Aztec text but is here translated and used as a footnote. — *The translators*)

The wall was thrown down in various places; the road was left clear.

Now that the area was clear, the Spaniards' various allied people quickly proceeded to fill each canal.

The horsemen passed over, following after the others.

Some Tlatelolcans came encountering the horsemen, who speared one.

On the ground they repeatedly struck him on the back of the head.

All the brave warriors jumped ashore from the boats in which they had been fighting while the young boys poled them.

There were volleys of stones on both sides.

They left their gun on the gladiatorial sacrificial stone. We warriors seized it.

70

VII

MEXICO UNDER SIEGE

IN THEIR dread of the Spaniards the people of Tenochtitlan began to pour into Tlatelolco. There were wails and weeping; there was shouting. Many were the tears of the poor women. We men each took our women; some of us carried our children upon our shoulders. It took an entire day for the people of Tenochtitlan to abandon their city.

But the Tlatelolcans kept returning to Tenochtitlan to fight.

At about this time Pedro de Alvarado was already on the move against Ilyacac, which is over toward Nonoalco. He could do nothing; it was as if he were coming against a stone, for the Tlatelolcans were exerting themselves powerfully. There was fighting on the road and, in the shield-boats, on the water. Since Alvarado was just tiring himself out, he then turned back to establish himself again in Tlacopan.

But just two days later, when the first two brigantines came there — which we Mexicans repulsed — they then all assembled and set up camp near the houses of Nonoalco. From there they advanced on dry land. They followed the narrow road among the houses and reached the very center.

First all was clear there; none of the common folk came out. Then Tzilacatzin, a very brave warrior, came forth with three great, huge stones, one in his hand, two carried upon his shield. They were white wall stones. He cast them and thereupon pursued the Spaniards, scattering them and dispersing them into the water. They were soaked.

The brave Tzilacatzin was of the Otomí class of warriors. The Otomí style of hair-do was his by right. He despised his foes, even if they were Spaniards; he completely despised them. He inspired terror. When they saw Tzilacatzin, they cowered. And persistently did they seek to kill him, trying to transfix him with an iron bolt or to fell him with a gun shot. But Tzilacatzin just disguised himself, so that he would not be recognized. Sometimes he put on a device, hung his pendants on his lips, inserted his golden ear plugs, and put on his necklace of white shells. Only he left his head uncovered, so that it would be known that he was a warrior of the Otomí class. Sometimes he wore only his quilted cotton armor and a thin band about his forehead. Or sometimes he would disguise himself in a feather headdress with a wig, with two eagle feather pendants tied to the back of his head. This was the dress of one of the men who cast sacrificial victims into the fire in honor of the old fire god. He acted like one of the men who cast victims into the fire; he imitated his actions. His golden arm bands glistened on each arm; gold and leather leg bands shone on each leg. He was quite brilliant.

Tzilacatzin came forth with three great, huge stones.

The brave Tzilacatzin was of the Otomí class of warriors. He inspired terror.

And persistently did they seek to kill him.

Alvarado turned back to establish himself again in Tlacopan.

72

The day after having been chased into the water, the Spaniards sailed their boats again, grounding them at Nonoalco and at Ayauhcaltitlan, and brought in a great force of warriors on foot, including all the Tlaxcallans and the Otomí tribesmen. The Spaniards had indeed massed to try to overcome

Sometimes he put on a device, hung pendants on his lips, inserted his golden ear plugs, and put on his necklace of white shells. Sometimes he wore only his quilted cotton armor and a thin band about his forehead. Sometimes he would disguise himself in a feather headdress with a wig, with two eagle feather pendants.

us Mexicans. On their reaching Nonoalco, violent fighting broke out. On both sides there were deaths. Our foes were shot with arrows; Mexicans were shot with arrows. On both sides equally there were wounds. Thus was the fighting all through the day, all through the night.

Only three of the great brave warriors consistently refused to turn their faces away from the enemy, altogether despising them, setting no value upon the safety of their bodies. One was named Tzayectzin; the second, Temoctzin; the third, the warrior already described, Tzilacatzin.

Finally, tired out and unsuccessful in trying to break us, the Spaniards, considerably afflicted, withdrew to their quarters followed by their allies.

Once it came to pass that the floating gardens people, the Xochimilcans, Cuitlauacans, Itztapalapanians, Mizquicans, Colhuacanians, Mexicaltzincans, and others sent messengers to Mexico as if they wanted to help us. They came to confer with Quauhtemoc,[1] new ruler of Mexico, and his lords and brave warriors. They said to these, "Beloved noblemen, we have come with a little help for the city. This is the message of our rulers, who keep watch where we came from, though in truth the real rulers are here. Our eagle warriors, our jaguar warriors have come; they are assembled in boats. They will now expel the enemy."

[1] Cuitlauac had died of smallpox and Quauhtemoc became the eleventh and last ruler of the Mexicans.

73

The floating gardens people, the Xochimilcans, and others sent messengers to Mexico.

They came to confer with Quauhtemoc, new ruler of Mexico, and his lords.

The Spaniards sailed their boats again, grounding them at Nonoalco. Violent fighting broke out.

Only three of the brave warriors consistently refused to turn their faces away.

74

The messengers having spoken, the Mexican leaders consulted among themselves and then answered them: "Very well. We are obliged to you. You have tired yourselves; you are weary. Help the city; see what can be done."

Then they gave all of them shields, emblems, and chocolate, broad gourds full of chocolate. Then they said to them, "Take courage! Attempt it, brave warriors; our enemies are upon us." And the Cuitlauacan messengers and others went escorted by Mexicans to the battle, which extended roaring all along the road. There was then fighting.

But the Xochimilcans with a yell threw themselves on the boats. They were not here to give us aid but to rob the people. They kidnapped the women, young and old, and the children. Some they there killed; others they spared, calmly lowering them into their boats.

As they were doing this, when they had already treacherously brought harm to the people, the seasoned warriors saw them and shouted: "Mexicans! Why do the villains do this? Pursue them!"

Then with a shout the Mexicans took after them in their boats; all the boats which lay at Nonoalco together left in pursuit. They closed in on the Xochimilcans, speared them, struck them repeatedly, killed them or took them captive. They indeed annihilated them. None of the captured women did the Xochimilcans succeed in kidnapping.

Just as the Xochimilcans had conceived, so would they have done; they would have destroyed us by treachery.

All the captives we took in this engagement, the Xochimilcans, Cuitlauacans, etc., we forced back to Yacacolco, later site of the Church of Santa Ana, where stood Quauhtemoc and Mayeuatzin, the ruler of Cuitlauac.[2] The captives loitered to greet Mayeuatzin: "Brother," they said, "farewell!" But he said, "You villains! Did I tell you to come? What have you been doing?" Quauhtemoc said to him, "Brother, do your duty"; and Mayeuatzin at once offered up four of them as sacrifices. Quauhtemoc also killed four. Later it was ordered that all the captives be sacrificed everywhere in the temples.

And we Mexicans remained angry. We said, "The Xochimilcans live near us; they mingle with us; they have made their homes here. Do they take information to the enemy? We shall abandon them; they will perish." The women and youths were freed, but all the rest were killed, every one. None were spared, for it had been as if they bore false witness against us when they brought undeserved harm pretending to help us.

After some days two brigantines came drawing in to Yauhtenco. This was the only activity the Spaniards showed. They sailed in at early dawn. Having beached their boats, they came ashore firing guns and shooting crossbow bolts. We warriors remained crouching low at the walls or hidden among the houses. A sentinel watched, estimating the best time to break out in a charge against them.

[2] He was here at the time that war broke out, and had stayed. (This remark appears as an "aside" in the Aztec text but is here translated and used as a footnote. — The translators)

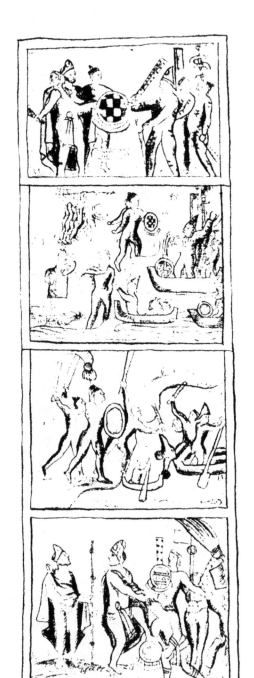

Mayeuatzin at once offered up four of them as sacrifices. Quauhtemoc also killed four.

After some days two brigantines came drawing in to Yauhtenco.

They gave all of them shields, emblems, and chocolate.

They kidnapped the women, young and old, and the children.

With a shout the Mexicans took after them in their boats.

All the captives we forced back to Yacacolco where stood Quauhtemoc and Mayeuatzin.

At the right moment he called out, "Courage, Mexicans!" He brandished his shield, and with a yell and the sounding of shell trumpets, we warriors took after the Spaniards and knocked down and took eighteen of them. The enemy withdrew their boats to the middle of the lake.

As they lay watching, the eighteen were forced to Tlacochcalco, the place of the spear house, where they were to die. We stripped them of all their war array, their quilted cotton armor, all that was on them; we completely stripped them, made slaves of them, and killed them as sacrifices.

At another time the Spaniards forced two of their boats into Xocotitlan, beached them, and went to look at the people and the hamlet. Tzilacatzin and some other brave warriors saw the Spaniards and ran forward against them, throwing stones at them. The Spaniards scattered into the water.

Then again they sailed to Coyonacazco, to fight there. As they beached, some Spaniards came out led by Xicotencatl Castañeda carrying his quetzal feather ball emblem. They shot crossbow bolts, but hit only one — in the forehead, so that he died. It was Castañeda's shot. But the brave warriors dashed at him and drove the Spaniards back into the water, continuing to throw stones at them. Castañeda would have been killed, but he clung to one of the boats, and they carried him back to Xocotitlan.

One boat was kept at Tetenantepotzco, where the walls curve; another they kept at Totecco, where the road leads direct to Tepetzinco. Here the enemy were continuously on guard, though they removed the boat at night.

Some days later the Spaniards came to a decision about us and advanced. They had come upon the Quauecatitlan road going straight to the place where salt is sold. At that point they gathered together, and every Tlaxcallan, Acolhuacanian, and Chalcan began filling the canal. Where they could not go they threw in adobes, house beams, door lintels, posts, and logs; they even tied bunches of reeds together and threw them into the water. When they had filled it, the Spaniards took up their formation and cautiously started marching. The standard led them; they blew trumpets and beat drums. Following them came Tlaxcallans and other allies, the Tlaxcallans making a great effort, shaking their heads, beating their breasts, singing.

We Mexicans also sang; we all sang whatever we remembered; we encouraged ourselves.

So the enemy came to reach Tlalhuacan. There the brave Mexican warriors lay well crouched, well hidden, waiting for the proper instant, when they would hear the shouting to rise against the invaders — when they would be sent to meet them.

At another time the Spaniards forced two of their boats into Xocotitlan.

When the shout arose — "Courage, Mexicans!" — then Tlapanecatl Ecatzin, of the Otomí class of warriors, threw himself upon the foe. "Courage, brave warriors! Courage, Tlatelolcans! Who are these savages? On with you!" With this, he struck a Spaniard down to the ground. This Ecatzin was the first to knock one down; others dragged him off.

On this, we warriors crouching hidden all together cast ourselves on the Spaniards and forced them to run among the houses. When they realized what was happening, they acted just like drunk men. We overtook them; we slew or captured them in abundance. Many Spaniards, Tlaxcallans, Acolhuans, Texcocans, Chalcans, Xochimilcans, etc., were taken. And in slaying them we indeed forced the Spaniards and their allies into the lake.

For the road had become too slippery to walk on. The men continually slipped and slid. The captives were dragged along it by force. Here, too, where it is now called San Martín, the Spaniards' banner was seized from them; Tlatelolcan warriors took it. But the enemy ignored the loss of the flag; they gave it no heed.

Some Spaniards escaped. We Mexicans withdrew leaving them exhausted at Colhuacatonco, by the side of the canal. There the surviving Spaniards gathered themselves together.

Then we took the captives to Yacacolco, rounding them up, forcing them to go. One would weep, another sing, another yell while striking his mouth with the palm of his hand. . . . At Yacacolco we ranged them in rows. One by one they were marched to the

Castañeda would have been killed, but he clung to one of the boats.

One boat was kept at Tetenantepotzco, where the walls curve; another they kept at Totecco, where the road leads direct to Tepetzinco.

Tlapanecatl Ecatzin, of the Otomí class of warriors, struck a Spaniard down to the ground.

78

The Spaniards' banner was seized from them. Tlatelolcan warriors took it.

Some Spaniards escaped. We Mexicans withdrew.

We took the captives to Yacacolco.

small pyramid to be sacrificed to the gods. The Spaniards were taken care of first; then the warriors from the allied cities. When they had been killed, then we strung each Spaniard's head on the upper part of the skull rack;[3] below we strung the heads of the captured horses. All were arranged to face the sun. None of the heads of the Spaniards' allies were placed on the skull rack.

Fifty-three Spaniards and four horses were taken.

Not because of this success did watchfulness relax. The Xochimilcans surrounded us everywhere with their boats. Fighting continued, both sides took captives, on both sides there were deaths.

Nevertheless, great became the suffering of the common folk. There was hunger. Many died of famine. There was no more good, pure water to drink — only nitrous water. Many died of it — contracted dysentery which killed them. The people ate anything — lizards, barn swallows, corn leaves, saltgrass; they gnawed colorin wood, glue orchid, the frilled flower; or leather and buckskin, cooked or toasted; or sedum and adobe bricks. Never had such suffering been seen; it was terrifying how many of us died when we were shut in as we were.

And quite imperturbably the enemy pressed about us like a wall; quite imperturbably they herded us.

---

[3] The skull rack, *tzompantli*, was a structure located near the principal temples. See illustration.

We strung each Spaniard's head on the upper part of the skull rack; below we strung the heads of the captured horses.

The Spaniards were taken care of first. . . .

Then the warriors from the allied cities.

VIII

THE BEGINNING OF THE END

Then the Spaniards began to harass us in Tlatelolco. The first time they penetrated the market place here was once when four horsemen broke in and galloped around the edge of the area, lancing the brave warriors. They killed a good many. This was the first time; then they withdrew, turning their backs on us. Our brave warriors were fearless against them; they took after the Spaniards.

Their attack was unexpected; there was no warning.

This was the time, too, that they burned the temple. They set fire to it; it burst into flames, the tongues of fire rising high, crackling, and continually flaring up. There was weeping, there were tears among the Tlatelolcans, who expected that the people would then be plundered.

For a long time fighting continued in the market place. Battles were fought at each of its edges. Gradually the Tlatelolcans were made to abandon the wall of Tenexnamacoyan, where lime was sold, and at Copalnamacoyan, where incense was sold; then the Spaniards could penetrate among the houses at Xochicalco. Somehow the brave warriors managed to be everywhere on the walls thereabouts, for all of the houses of the Quauhquechollan area surrounding the market place became a wall, and many warriors lay out of sight on the roof terraces, from which they could throw stones and shoot arrows. Besides, the warriors had made small openings in the back of the Quauhquechollan houses; when the horsemen followed after anyone, when they tried to kick him or to get ahead of him, he would slip inside.

When the Spaniards entered Acatl iyacapan, then there was plundering and capturing of the common folk, until our brave warriors saw what was going on and repulsed the enemy warriors. It happened that one of our shorn-hair warriors, named Axoquentzin, was standing there. He took after the enemy; he made them let the people go and turn tail. But he died there; the Spaniards shot him through the heart with an iron crossbow bolt. As if stretched out in sleep he lay dead.

Then the enemy sat down to rest.

They penetrated the market place and galloped around the edge of the area.

There similarly was combat there at Ya-cacolco. The crossbowmen came filing in order. With them arrived allied warriors supplied by the Four Lords. Their object was to close off the road. As the sun began to hang low, our brave warriors were crouching low among the houses in order to join battle with them. But when they had done this, some of our foes climbed a roof terrace, saw us, and called out, "Ho, Tlaxcallans! This way! Here they are!" Then they rained darts upon us and crumbled us.

Thus the Spaniards slowly reached Yaca-colco, carrying battle to each edge. But they were receiving more hurt than they gave; they could not break through the Tlatelolcans, who remained across the water stoning them, shooting arrows at them. No ford nor bridge did the enemy take.

This was the time that they burned the temple.

The Spaniards shot him through the heart with an iron crossbow bolt.

Warriors lay out of sight on the roof terraces, from which they could throw stones and shoot arrows.

Here the illustrations break off in the original version of this account, although spaces were left in the manuscript for two or three dozen more, presumably because of haste in trying to complete the manuscript for delivery to Spanish civil and ecclesiastical authorities.

82

I nic icmpoalli onea cibilli coma nic capitelo: vncan mih a ing ijie. Heria incoinvelada in quitlatiapcaia in ati icioaltia, in vnian atquijtui Spanoles in tlaca—.

By day the Spaniards systematically filled in the canals. By night, when the foe had withdrawn, we Mexicans with continual difficulty uncovered them. When dawn came, the scene looked just as it had the day before. For when the Spaniards had filled the canals, we at once took out the stones, the wood, etc. Thus by a little we lengthened the war. Only with difficulty could the Spaniards cross; the canals were our great walls.

In closing in on us, the Spaniards and the Tlaxcallans concentrated upon the highway to Yacacolco and Atezcapan. The Xochimilcans, Cuitlauacans, Mizquicans, Colhuacanians, and Itztapalapanians gave their attention to Yacacolco, Cuepopan, Apauazcan, Atliceuhyan, Ayacac, and Totecco. They undertook to give battle in boats.

On the other hand, the warriors of Atlicuehyan and Ayacac, both boatmen and bowmen, lost no time in readying themselves to resist the Spaniards and Tlaxcallans. For a time they held their own. Barbed spears rained down like rattlesnakes striking, so did the arrows hit their mark. When they used their dart throwers, it was as if the mass of darts cast a yellow shadow over the enemy.

Some of the brave warriors — Xiuhcozcatzin, Quaquatzin, Uitzitzin, and Itzcuin-

tzin, lesser noblemen who lived in Yacacolco — lost no time in saving their women and children. They went to great pains to arrange protection for them by another canal, in Amaxac.

And once the Spaniards landed in Totecco; when they came to the buildings where the young were trained as warriors, they set fire to them. Another of the brigantines entered at Atliceuhyan accompanied by boats full of Xochimilcans. Brave Temilotzin, a warrior who had distinguished himself by taking four captives, was standing erect on a small pyramid facing the Spaniards. Then brave Coyoueuetzin, dressed in the array of an eagle-jaguar warrior, half eagle, half jaguar, came in a boat from Tolmayecan to throw the enemy back. He brought many shield-boats with him. "Courage, brave warriors," he shouted; "we are repulsing them!" And they fell upon the enemies' boats. When the Spaniards saw them, they turned and ran, the Mexicans pursuing them, Coyoueuetzin and his warriors then going to Atliceuhyan. Many Xochimilcans fell under Mexican arrows. The Spaniards then withdrew their boats to Amanalco, where they lined them up. Those pursued by the Mexicans made a stand. Coyoueuetzin hid behind a small pyramid, and then with his brave warriors reversed the enemy. He forced them to the young warriors' school in Atliceuhyan. Then the Spaniards turned on Coyoueuetzin, chased him, and made him jump into the water. But then Itzpapalotzin, a young warrior of the Otomí class, in turn repelled the Spaniards. Putting on a device, he drove them off — rolled them up like mud balls, forced them

83

into their boats, so that they went off defeated.

In this confusion the Cuitlauacan warriors thought their ruler Mayeuatzin had fallen among those who had died. They were very angry. "You have killed our ruler," they clamored. "Bring him to us! Why have you killed our ruler?" Mayeuatzin, seeing that his men were angry, in turn became angry himself. He turned to Coyoueuetzin and said, "Brother, call up one of our brave warriors who can shout loudly, who has a strong voice." They called Tlamayocatl, a seasoned warrior. Mayeuatzin then commanded him, "Go there. Tell the Cuitlauacans this: 'Cuitlauacans, your ruler Mayeuatzin has sent me. Look! There he stands, on the small pyramid!' " The Cuitlauacans heard him, but they said, "No! You have killed him!" Tlamayocatl shouted, "He is not dead! Look! There he stands!" And Mayeuatzin also called out, "I am not dead! Nothing has damaged even my lip pendant, my jadeite, my emblem!" But as he finished, with a roar from the Spaniards' allies the fighting broke out anew; they turned on and gave chase to the Mexicans. It lasted long in the market place, at the place where incense used to be sold, and then gradually ceased.

Another time our enemies from Tliliuhquitepec and Atetemollan decided upon a joint attempt. They already knew the path which led among the houses, belonging to a nobleman called Tlacotzin. Our foes entered through it. Then our brave warriors took after them. Among ours was a personage named Tlapanecatl, a seasoned warrior from Atezcapan; he contended notably against the enemy. They seized him. Our men hurled themselves upon him to rescue him, shot volleys of arrows, and made his captors release him. They had wounded him in that part of the calf of the leg which is penitentially bled,[1] but the foe abandoned the fight and withdrew.

In icconpul, in ai t vil onci aquitui: uua' xoba mi u cu in Spanoles quj tla lque quawito matlah, injecqupi ji lonjiii yeya jn iat lui i.

Then the Spaniards tried setting up a catapult with which they could treacherously stone the common folk. When they had erected it, when they were about to use it, they kept circling about it and there was much pointing with their fingers. They pointed at the people — pointed to Amaxac, where the common folk were assembled. They stretched out their arms as if they were going to shoot it, as if they were going to use a sling on them. Then they turned to wind the ropes. The beam of the catapult rose upright. But the stone fell far short of the people it was to hit; it reached only to the back of the market place at Xomolco.

There consequently developed a dispute among the Spaniards; it looked as if they

---

[1] The word in the Aztec text is "thigh," but the act itself was performed upon the calf of the leg. Among the Aztecs' penitential acts was the bleeding of the calf of the leg or of other parts of the body; the blood was offered to one or another of the gods.

84

were poking at one another's faces with their fingers. There was a great deal of jabbering. And the catapult's beam kept moving back and forth, teetering from one side to the other. Gradually it balanced itself vertically. Then it could be seen that at its point was its sling. Its ropes were very thick. Because of them the Mexicans called it the wooden sling.

The Spaniards and Tlaxcallans again descended upon us Mexicans. They drew up in order in Yacacolco, Tecpancaltitlan, and Copalnamacoyan. Then, at Atecocolecan, the Spaniards very slowly led those who were beseiging us. Our Mexican warriors too took their places, each one animated and exalted as to his manhood; none cowardly, none acting like women. "Come on, brave warriors," they called out. "Who are these little savages? Who are these barbarians?" And they went off zig-zagging, one side to the other, for none walked straight nor raised himself erect.

And the Spaniards would often disguise themselves, in order not to show themselves as they were. They dressed as we did. They put on our war array and fastened our capes over themselves in order not to be distinguished. They often came up to and mingled with a group of us; we realized they were there when they shot an arrow at one of us. Everyone crouched; everyone fell to the ground. Everyone always carefully watched where the bolt came from and where it went. Very careful, very cautious were the brave Tlatelolcan warriors.

Still, the Spaniards gradually drove us back, pressed us back against the houses. At Copalnamacoyan, where the incense used to be sold, and at Amaxac they were practically shield to shield against us.

It was at Amaxac that a Tlatelolcan named Chalchiuhtepeua hid himself behind a house where he could closely study one of the horses to see how he could best spear it. He speared it, and the Spanish rider was thrown to the ground. Each of his friends ran to pick him up; all our brave warriors and noblemen came forth and chased the horsemen off, and continued to harry their rear guard. Then they once more made them take a stand at Copalnamacoyan, at the wall. Then there was a lull; the fighters went off each to his own home.

One early dawn all the Spaniards' allies crowded at Teteuhtitlan to fill a pond named Tlaixcuepan. They threw in all manner of rocks, wood, pillars, door lintels, adobes, corner stones, and so on, chattering among themselves and raising a great dust. They planned to rob the people living in this border area, the road leading to Tepeyacac.

When the brave Mexican warriors noticed what was going on and realized why, they too laid plans. In due course a boat approached, very cautiously poled, up to the edge of the road. It was covered over; no warlike gear showed. Then another boat was cautiously poled up. Then two more came up. There were now four of them.

Suddenly there appeared in them two eagle warriors and two jaguar warriors — respectively, Tepantemoctzin and Tlacotzin, and Temilotzin and Coyoueuetzin. Then another jaguar and eagle pair of warriors appeared. Poling, they made the boats fly through the water, going cautiously, however, to Teteuhtitlan to head the enemy off—

to cut them off. Then they were followed by another eagle and jaguar pair of warriors. They were to jump on the enemy. The people were robbed, but some warriors who had come from a distance succeeded in cutting off the looters.

When the enemy saw this, it was too late for most of them to flee. Many fell into the water, pulling in others with them, and drowning. They were stunned with surprise, as if unconscious, as if suddenly soaked. Some fell into the spaces between beams used to fill the pond; those who were pulled out were completely covered, soaked, gleaming with mud. But many perished.

This was the only time that our enemies, that is, the Spaniards' allies, died in large numbers there. Next day after this carnage it was quite quiet.

When the Spaniards took Amaxac, when the people were finished, they had indeed succeeded in surrounding us. Battle raged at every edge, especially at Amaxac and the road to Tepeyacac. They entered the young men's warrior training school at Ueican, because the young men were gathered there. When they ascended to the roof terrace, the people, who were scattered behind the young men's house, dispersed quickly into the water. A great shorn-hair warrior, Uitzilhuatzin, got up onto a roof terrace overlooking the young men's house; strong as a wall himself, he attracted some support on the part of the people. The Spaniards at once attacked them and fell upon them, succeeding in striking, cutting, and pounding Uitzilhuatzin. He was rescued by other brave warriors, who drove the Spaniards off,

though they tried to capture him. He could not die. So the Spaniards withdrew.

The area was deserted for a time. But the Spaniards had burned the images of the gods — all of them. The brave warriors were still hopelessly resisting. The Spaniards were at least not shooting the women, unless they were playing the part of men. When each side withdrew, it was late afternoon.

The fourth day was the same. The enemy moved together; where the people were, the Spaniards penetrated slowly, with great caution. Brave Temilotzin — he had taken four captives — was watching from behind a wall. He ran out arrayed as an eagle warrior. He had an iron sword, and started out to cut the enemy off, but saw that it was no use, and so threw himself into the canal with a burst of water. There was a great yell from the men, and battle again raged at each edge. All day it raged.

At dawn on the fifth day our enemies, the Spaniards and their allies, attacked us in force. They all surrounded us. They all moved together. They wound themselves, wrapped themselves around us. No one could go anywhere. We jostled and crowded against one another. Many, in fact, died trampled in the press. When the enemy came close to us, there was one woman who threw water at their heads; it ran down their faces.

Then the ruler Quauhtemoc and the brave warriors Coyoueuetzin, Temilotzin, Topantemoctzin, Tlacotzin, Petlauhtzin, and the judge Auelitoctzin determined upon a great, brave warrior called Tlapaltecatl opochtzin, a Coatlan man. They put the quetzal-owl garb upon him, array which had once belonged to the ruler Auitzotl.

"This array was the array of my dear father Auitzotl. Let this warrior wear it; let him die in it," said Quauhtemoc. "May he vaunt himself in it before the enemy; let him show himself to them in it. Let the enemy see it; let them wonder at it!"

When they had dressed him in it, he was frightening, wonderful to behold. They bade four other warriors go with him to help, and they furnished him with darts which had belonged to the god — rod-like darts with flint points. With this array it was as if he had become one of the class of Mexico's rulers.

"Mexicans! Tlatelolcans!" the deputy ruler Tlacotzin said. "Is there nothing left of the Mexican state? What we have here is what naturally belongs to the god Uitzilopochtli — the weapons he cast. These are the fire serpent and the fire drill which he hurled at our enemies. What you wield, Mexicans, is the dart which is naturally his. Make it turn toward our enemies. Do not drop it; throw it with force against them. If one or two of our enemies are hit, Uitzilopochtli is truly on our side. We shall find his favor for a while. What more will he require?"

Then the quetzal-owl figure went off, his quetzal feathers spreading.

When the enemy saw him, it was as if a mountain had split in pieces. The Spaniards were terrified; he frightened them; he was something to wonder at.

He got up on a roof terrace. Some of the enemy who could see him came against him, turned him back, and gave him chase. Then he turned upon and pursued them; he took their quetzal feathers and gold from them. Then he sprang down from the roof terrace. He did not die and the enemy did not capture him; rather, three or four enemies had been taken.

Finally the battle just quietly ended. Silence reigned. Nothing happened. The enemy left. All was quiet, and nothing more took place. Night fell, and the next day nothing happened, either. No one spoke aloud; the people were crushed. Nor did the Spaniards move; they remained still, looking at the people. Nothing was happening.

Following are the brave warriors, the great war leaders, who commanded and presided over the war. The Tlatelolcans were the high warriors Coyoueuetzin and the lord of Tzilacan, Temilotzin. Those of Tenochtitlan were the ruler's deputy Tlacotzin and the high judge Motelchiuhtzin. These were the great brave warriors of Tlatelolco and Tenochtitlan.

IX

THE END

Late that night a sign appeared which made it clear that we were forced to the wall with no hope of relief. It had rained or sprinkled at intervals. Then, in the deepest darkness of the night there appeared in the heavens what was like a fiery bloodstone continually spinning, revolving, in a flaming whirlwind. Then the blazing, turning ember seemed to split into fragments, some large, some small, some only sparks. It swung up like a coppery wind, swishing, cracking, popping as it circled the ramparts at the lake shore and rocketed toward Coyonacazco. There it plunged into the water and was no more.

No one called out; no one yelled striking the lips with the hand. No one said anything.

Next day nothing happened. We lay quiet; our enemies lay quiet.

Cortés could be seen watching from under a many-hued canopy on Aztauatzin's house, in Amaxac. He was looking toward the people crowded in Tlatelolco. About him swarmed Spaniards; they were consulting among themselves.

On our side were Quauhtemoc and the rest of our leaders: the deputy ruler Tlacotzin; the high judge Motelchiuhtzin; the chief priest; the high warrior Petlauhtzin. These represented Tenochtitlan. Representing Tlatelolco were the high warriors Coyoueuetzin, Temilotzin, Topantemoctzin; Uitzitzin, a lesser nobleman; and the high judges Auelitoctzin and Uitziliuitzin. All of these were rulers. They had gathered in Tolmayecan to decide among themselves how to offer tribute and submission to the Spaniards.

After a while Quauhtemoc left in a boat with two companions, his personal page Yaztachimal and the brave warrior Tepotzitoloc. The boat was poled by Cenyaotl.

The people wept as they saw them go. "Already noble young Quauhtemoc is leaving to surrender himself to the gods, the Spaniards!"

They captured him and disembarked him, all looking on as they took him by the arm to draw him forth. Then they escorted him to the roof top to present him to Cortés, who first stroked Quauhtemoc with his hand and then had him sit by him. Then they fired a volley from their guns --- striking no one, for they just fired upward so that the shots passed over our heads.

Then they brought out a gun, put it into a boat, and carried it to the house of Coyoueuetzin; they set it upon the roof terrace and fired it at the people. Many died. And the Mexicans just ran away.

So ended the war. When the shields were laid down, when we gave in, it was in the year Three House of the civil calendar's count and the day One Serpent of the ceremonial calendar's count.

Then a shout arose: "Enough! Now we can leave! We can go out and eat greens!" This was the signal for the people to leave — though they could only go into the water; for some, starting off along the great road, clashed with and killed some of the allies of the Spaniards. This, and the fact that some of those leaving went armed with shields and obsidian-bladed swords, aroused the enemy's anger.

Those who set out from the groups of houses still standing went straight to Amaxac, where the road divided. From there some went to Tepeyacac, some to Xoxouiltitlan, some to Nonoalco. None could go toward Xoloco nor to Mazatzintamalco. Those who depended upon boats or lived in houses raised on piles, as well as the people of Tolmayecan, had to take to the water. Some walked, the water reaching to their chests or their necks — if they did not indeed drown. The little children rode their elders' backs. Some people had boats. Though most fled by night, striking against one another as they poled, some left by daylight. There arose tearful wails — though some left rejoicing, in some contentment.

But on the roads the Spaniards stopped the people everywhere, mostly to rob them. They despised jadeite, turquoise, precious feathers; they looked for gold. They sought it in our clothing — in the poor women's bosoms, in their skirts; in the breech cloths of us men. They opened and looked into our mouths.

And they seized and kept some of the fugitives, mostly our pretty women, the yellow-skinned ones; so that some, afraid they might be taken, would muddy their faces and clothe themselves in rags. But also they took some of us men, the strong ones, youths maturing into manhood, those suitable later to become their messengers, their servants. On some they branded the cheeks. On some they painted a mark on the cheek or the lips.

After Quauhtemoc had surrendered himself, the Spaniards took him at night to Acachinanco. But next day they came again to the scene of battle, many of them, in battle array, wearing their iron breast and back pieces and iron helmets, though carrying neither their iron shields nor their iron swords. All of them pressed white handkerchiefs against their noses, for the stench of the dead, which was strong, sickened them.

Some of them walked holding, by their capes, besides Quauhtemoc, Coanacochtzin, ruler of Texcoco, and Tetlepanquetzatzin, ruler of Tlacopan. Only these three were held; not the ruler's deputy Tlacotzin, the high warrior Petlauhtzin, the high judge Motelchiuhtzin, the chief priest, the lord of priests Coatzin, the keeper Tlazolyaotzin, and those who guarded all the gold.

They went direct to Acatzinco, to the house of the high warrior, brave Coyoueuetzin, the Spaniards advancing in two long files. Reaching the house, they climbed up to the roof terrace and sat down, first setting up a canopy made of a many-hued cape for Cortés. There he sat; near him was Marina.

Nearby also were the captive leaders. Quauhtemoc had put on the shining cape of century plant fiber, each half of different color, all ornamented with hummingbird feathers after the fashion of the Ocuillanians. The cape was dirty; it was all he had. Next was Coanacochtzin, ruler of Texcoco, dressed only in a century plant fiber cape with a design of radiating flowers and a flowered border. It too was dirty. Then came Tetlepanquetzatzin, ruler of Tlacopan. He too wore a very dirty century plant fiber cape. And there were also the judge Auelitoctzin and a nobleman, Yopicatl popocatzin of Tlatelolco. On one side were captive dignitaries of Tenochtitlan: Tlacotzin, Petlauhtzin, Motelchiuhtzin, the chief priest, the lord of priests Coatzin, and the keeper Tlazolyaotl.

I njc ompoalli oce capitulo vnca myłva intlatulli injc quinzonzolz do hernando cor fes injxquichtin altepetl ipa' tlatoque innjcan Mexico: auh Tezcuco, Tlacuba, injquac ieo moman chimalli, inqujntemo haia in cuztic teucujtlatl, in vn con qujcen mantiqujsque tul taca acaluco, injquac qujzque, cho loque mexico.

This was the group which Cortés, through Marina, questioned as to the gold lost in the Tolteca canal as the Spaniards were fleeing from Mexico.

"What of the gold?" Cortés asked the Mexican rulers. "What of the gold guarded in Mexico?"

At this point all the gold was removed from the boats and laid before Cortés: indeed all of it, the golden flags, the golden conical caps, the bands for the arm and for the calf of the leg, the helmets, the discs. . . .

"Is this absolutely all the gold kept here in Mexico?" Cortés then asked. "You will show it all. You will seek it all."

"Let the lord, the god listen," said Tlacotzin. "This was taken to our palace; we kept it hidden behind a blank adobe wall. Didn't our lords in fact take it all with them?"

Marina explained, "Cortés says, 'Yes, we took it all. It was all gathered together and marked. But you made us leave it there at the Tolteca canal; you made us drop it. You must produce all of that gold.'"

"Let the god, let Cortés listen," the ruler's deputy Tlacotzin continued. "The warriors of Tenochtitlan do not take to boats; it is not one of their accomplishments. It is an attribute of the Tlatelolcans, who fight in boats. They came to stop our lords as they fled. Didn't the Tlatelolcans in fact take it all?"

Here Quauhtemoc turned to the ruler's deputy. "What are you saying, ruler's deputy? Even if the Tlatelolcans did take it, were not those who did so arrested? Didn't they give it all up? Wasn't it gathered together in Texopan? And what did our lords have with them as they left if not this?"

He pointed to the gold.

"Cortés asks if this is absolutely all of it," Marina said to him.

"Perhaps some of the people got away with some," the ruler's deputy said. "It will be found. Our lord Cortés will have it."

"Cortés says," Marina once again broke in, " 'You will deliver two hundred pieces of gold this size' " — indicating a circle with her hands.

Once more the ruler's deputy interjected, "Maybe some poor woman hid it in her skirts. It will be found. He will have it."

Then the high judge Auelitoctzin spoke. "Let the nobleman, our lord Cortés, listen. This is how our treasure was accumulated. When Moctezuma was still alive, when a conquest was made, the Mexicans, Tlatelolcans, Tepanecans, and Acolhuacanians campaigned together. All the Mexicans, all the Acolhuacanians, all the floating garden people, all of us campaigned together in a war of conquest.

"Then when the city fell, we returned, all separately, to our cities. Later the people of the conquered city came to us. They brought their tribute — the things which became the victors' goods: the jadeite, the gold, the precious feathers, the other precious stones, the fine turquoise, the lovely cotinga, the roseate spoonbill. . . . They gave it to Moctezuma; it came here together. All the tribute, all the gold, was together here in Tenochtitlan. . . ."

EPILOGUE

Here Sahagún's account breaks off. Although we cannot know the words with which it ended, a short account by Chimalpahin, a native chronicler from nearby Chalco, indicates Tlacotzin remarked that the Aztecs came into the Valley of Mexico landless, took land by force of arms as the Spaniards had just done, and were again landless through the fortunes of war, and that Cortés returned those lands to the former subject states. Whatever the importance or accuracy of Chimalpahin's account, we can be certain that the defeated Aztecs were expecting peace on the terms usual in the Mesoamerica of their time. If a city-state had submitted without fighting or with little resistance, it might become a lesser partner, more or less self-ruling but with light tribute payment imposed; if resistance had been strong or desperate, tribute exactions were onerous and the ruling class or family rigidly hampered or eliminated. What actually happened to them as a result of the Conquest they most certainly could not have foreseen: the incorporation of the conquered states into the Spanish imperial system and the constant expansion of the system until it reached its maximum extent and concentration. Much less could they have foreseen the colonies transformed into modern states. But the aftermath of the destruction of the Aztecs, the establishment and growth of New Spain, and the subsequent fate of the conquered natives, which are developments in colonial history, cannot be told here.

We know very little for certain of what befell the stalwart warriors who survived the destruction of Tenochtitlan. Temoctzin, one of "the three great brave warriors [who] consistently refused to turn their faces away from the enemy," surrendered to Cortés and eventually became governor of Tlatelolco. Ecatzin also was captured; he preceded Temoctzin as the first governor of Tlatelolco under Spanish rule. Topantemoctzin, Coyoueuetzin, and Temilotzin all survived; they died in Quauhtitlan. The last named lived until perhaps 1537, after having served his turn as governor of Tlatelolco. As for the others who had fought equally bravely and whose names Sahagún gives us, they are lost to us.

We do, however, know rather more concerning what finally befell some of the parties to this last interview. They were the ones whom the Spaniards at their convenience maintained as puppet kings of sorts. Of these, Quauhtemoc (of Tenochtitlan), Coanacochtzin (of Texcoco), and **Tetlepanquetza-tzin** (of Tlacopan) were allowed their former status—though not authority—until, in 1525, they were taken by Cortés on his unfortunate Honduras expedition and executed — or murdered, if you prefer — by Cortés for suspected treachery. To fill Quauhtemoc's office he elevated Tlacotzin, who, however, almost at once died; Motelchiuhtzin was then assigned his place, which he kept until he died in the Guzmán expedition in 1530. As for Marina, we know that during the Honduras expedition, Cortés gave her in marriage, though she was mother of his child, to a Spanish conquistador, don Juan Jaramillo. And Cortés, discontented with his reception in Spain, not permitted the rule of the vast domains he had conquered, and disappointed in his attempts to gain Charles V's favor, died in Spain in 1547.